MULTICULTURAL EDUCATION SERIES

James A. Banks, Series Editor

D0813709

RACE CULTURE AND **POLITICS** IN **EDUCATION**

A Global Journey from South Africa

KOGILA MOODLEY

Afterword by Sonia Nieto

TEACHERS COLLEGE PRESS

TEACHERS COLLEGE | COLUMBIA UNIVERSITY

NEW YORK AND LONDON

Published by Teachers College Press,® 1234 Amsterdam Avenue, New York, NY 10027

Library of Congress Cataloging-in-Publication Data is available at loc.gov

Names: Moodley, Kogila, author.
Title: Race, culture, and politics in education : a global journey from
   South Africa / Kogila Moodley ; afterword by Sonia Nieto.
Description: New York, NY : Teachers College Press, 2020. | Series:
   Multicultural education series | Includes bibliographical references and
   index.
Identifiers: LCCN 2020038671 | ISBN 9780807764886 (paperback) | ISBN
   9780807764893 (hardcover) | ISBN 9780807779330 (ebook)
Subjects: LCSH: Moodley, Kogila. | Anti-racism. | Multiculturalism. |
   Multicultural education. | East Indians—South Africa—Biography. |
   Sociologists—South Africa—Biography. |
   Sociologists—Canada—Biography.
Classification: LCC HM479 .M59 2020 | DDC 305.8—dc23
LC record available at https://lccn.loc.gov/2020038671

ISBN 978-0-8077-6488-6 (paper)
ISBN 978-0-8077-6489-3 (hardcover)
ISBN 978-0-8077-7933-0 (ebook)

Printed on acid-free paper
Manufactured in the United States of America

For Heribert
Without whom this journey would never have been the same.
And for so much more . . .

Contents

Series Foreword

Global migration is a defining characteristic of the 21st century. The number of international migrants living abroad reached approximately 272 million in 2019, an increase of 51 million since 2010 (United Nations, 2019a). International migrants made up about 3.5% of the estimated global population of 7.7 billion (United Nations, 2019b). As Stephen Castles (2017) writes, "Together with cross-border flows—of commodities, capital, intellectual property, and culture—human mobility is an integral part of globalization" (p. 4). Emerging research indicates that in the future "climate change will cause humans to move across the planet at an unprecedented, destabilizing scale" (Lustgarten, 2020).

Nationalism and globalization coexist in tension worldwide. Globalization challenges nationalism and national boundaries and prioritizes cosmopolitanism and cooperative work of nations to solve problems that cut across national boundaries such as global warming, climate change, and pandemics such as COVID-19. Virulent and pernicious nationalism has emerged in nations around the world within the last decade, including the United States, the United Kingdom, Hungary, Switzerland, and other European nations.

This new nationalism has mobilized angry populist groups, stimulated the rise of authoritarianism, targeted immigrant groups and ethnic groups of color, and was among the factors that led to the passage of the Brexit referendum in the United Kingdom to leave the European Union and to the rise of leaders such as Viktor Orbán in Hungary and Donald J. Trump in the United States. Trump advocated an "America first" foreign policy, and made racially insensitive statements about immigrant groups, which were interpreted by White nationalist groups as supportive of their mission (Gray, 2017). National borders became more salient and tenacious in 2020 when the COVID-19 pandemic imperiled nations around the world and many countries shut down their borders to slow the spread of the virus.

Because global migration is a salient and pervasive phenomenon in the world today, researchers, policymakers, teachers, and students need incisive and informative books and publications that chronicle it. This compelling book is the reflective memoir of a global migrant, teacher, scholar, and parent who has inhabited five nations and three continents: South Africa, the United States, Germany, Egypt, and Canada. Kogila Moodley's life and professional journey epitomize a global voyage that is not only challenging, but also enriching and edifying. Her ancestors immigrated to South Africa from India as indentured laborers, where her parents were born; her strong Indian identity, unwavering support of her parents, and diligence enabled her to become a high-achieving and confident student within the institutionalized racist structure in South Africa, where laws and customs were codified in the apartheid system. Writes Moodley: "This system of legalized racism dictated from birth to death one's life chances solely on the basis of race."

In 1963, Moodley attended an orientation program at Yale University prior to her 2-year stay at Michigan State University to earn a master's degree in sociology. This was her first major journey out of South Africa. Her stay in the United States was illuminating, liberating, and enhanced her intellectual growth as well as her political consciousness because her visit to the United States coincided with the heyday of the Black Civil Rights Movement of the 1960s. Moodley writes warmly about her stay at Yale University: "The month I spent there was one of the most memorable experiences. It was my first exposure to a society where I could sit where I wanted to, eat in any restaurant, and visit any theatre. There was no color bar, unlike the country I had just left."

When Moodley and her German fiancé, Heribert Adam, were expelled from South Africa, they moved to Germany. After spending almost a year in Germany they relocated to Vancouver, Canada so that Moodley could study for her PhD degree at the University of British Columbia. After moving to Vancouver, Moodley and Adam spent 2 years in Cairo at the American University and travelled widely in Israel, Lebanon, Syria, and Jordan. Their family is still peripatetic. Since the demise of apartheid in the 1980s, Moodley and Adam travel each year to South Africa to do research and visit family members. They also make occasional trips to Berlin and Frankfurt to visit Adam's family, friends, and colleagues.

In this much-needed and enlightening book Moodley, with the eye of a perceptive anthropologist, a rich sociological imagination, and the skills of a seasoned cultural theorist, describes many complex concepts that teachers will find helpful when planning and teaching lessons about global migration and diversity, such as *race, ethnic identity, nationalism, resilience, resistance, cosmopolitanism,* and *political literacy*. For example, despite the powerful and ubiquitous influence of apartheid that existed in all South African institutions during her early socialization, Moodley exercised *efficacy* and *resistance* and refused to view herself as a victim. Some of the incidents that Moodley describes in this book are sobering and enraging to the reader, such as when her family was forced to move from their home so that a White British immigrant family could move into it; when she and her German fiancé were forced to leave South Africa; and when she and her daughters (aged 11 and 14), who were raised in Canada, were refused service at a Durban, South Africa restaurant in 1984. During these incidents, Moodley epitomized efficacy and resistance rather than victimization.

A main tenet of this book is that marginalized and racialized minorities who live in a racially stratified system must resist it with efficacy, resiliency, and determination and not become victimized by it. Writes Moodley, "My comparative study transcends the usual focus on racialized minorities as victims. Instead it highlights the power of agency even under unfavorable conditions. Indians like many other minorities made their space utilizing the power of communal mobilization at the expense of individual aggrandizement."

Moodley describes valuable and practical lessons she has learned from her sojourns and residencies in five nations in the Conclusions section of Chapter 12. The astute pedagogical insights stated in the Conclusions, as well as throughout this engaging and highly readable book, provide principles and guidelines that can be used to effectively teach political literacy to students from diverse racial, ethnic, and cultural groups. Moodley defines *political literacy* as "the skills of inquiry needed to understand the ways in which power operates in democratic and autocratic social contexts. The aim is to acquire basic knowledge gained through a critical reading of the way institutions function and an understanding of how democracy works in practice at local, national, and global levels . . . . *The best job educators can do to combat racism is to ensure a global political literacy*" (emphasis added). Because of the pedagogical insights that Moodley describes about teaching political literacy, cosmopolitism, and functioning across nations and cultures, this book is a substantial contribution to the Multicultural Education Series.

The major purpose of the Multicultural Education Series is to provide preservice educators, practicing educators, graduate students, scholars, and policymakers with an interrelated and comprehensive set of books that summarizes and analyzes important research, theory, and practice related to the education of ethnic, racial, cultural, and linguistic groups in the United States and the education of mainstream students about diversity. The dimensions of multicultural education, developed by Banks (2004) and described in the *Handbook of Research on Multicultural Education* and in the *Encyclopedia of Diversity in Education* (Banks, 2012), provide the conceptual framework for the development of the publications in the Series. The dimensions are content integration, the knowledge construction process, prejudice reduction, equity pedagogy, and an empowering institutional culture and social structure. The books in the Multicultural Education Series provide research, theoretical, and practical knowledge about the behaviors and learning characteristics of students of color (Conchas & Vigil, 2012; Lee, 2007), language minority students (Gándara & Hopkins 2010; Valdés, 2001; Valdés, Capitelli, & Alvarez, 2011), low-income students (Cookson, 2013; Gorski, 2018), and other minoritized population groups, such as students who speak different varieties of English (Charity Hudley & Mallinson, 2011), and LGBTQ youth (Mayo, 2014).

A number of the books in the Multicultural Education Series focus on institutional and structural racism and ways to reduce it in educational institutions, which is a significant and timely topic because of the national and international protests and dialogues about institutionalized racism that began after George Floyd, a Black man in Minneapolis, died when a White police officer pressed his knee to Floyd's neck for more than eight minutes on May 25, 2020. These books include Özlem Sensoy and Robin DiAngelo's *Is Everyone Really Equal? An Introduction to Key Concepts in Social Justice Education* (2017, 2nd ed.); Gary Howard's *We Can't Teach What We Don't Know: White Teachers, Multiracial Schools* (2016,

3rd ed.); Jabari Mahiri's *Deconstructing Race: Multicultural Education Beyond the Color-Bind* (2017); Zeus Leonardo's *Race Frameworks: A Multidimensional Theory of Racism and Education* (2013); and Daniel G. Solórzano and Lindsay Pérez Huber's *Racial Microaggressions: Using Critical Race Theory in Education to Recognize and Respond to Everyday Racism* (2020).

Parts of this riveting book are painful and somber because of the explicit and powerful examples Moodley uses to illustrate institutional racism and apartheid in South Africa. However, the overarching message of this inspiring book is that an individual with a strong and clarified ethnic identity, robust family support, resiliency, diligence, and determination—and with specific institutional and structural support along their journey, such as the scholarship that Moodley received from the Institute of International Education in 1963 to pursue a Master's degree in sociology—can succeed against great odds. Moodley's efficacious and remarkable sojourn in five nations—as well as becoming an internationally renowned researcher and scholar—typifies the statement by Mary McLeod Bethune, the great African American educator, "Without faith, nothing is possible. With it, nothing is impossible" (Bethune, 1952).

I am especially pleased to welcome this book to the Multicultural Education Series because of the long personal and professional relationship I have had with Kogila Moodley for almost 40 years. Our relationship began when she invited me to travel from Seattle, Washington to Kamloops, British Columbia in 1982 to make a presentation in a course she was teaching for Simon Fraser University. In subsequent years, I have been enriched by our intellectual exchanges, and by the contributions that Moodley has made to conferences and meetings that I have organized and to publications I have edited, including the paper she and Adam wrote for the conference on diversity and citizenship education that I organized and chaired at the Rockefeller Foundation's Study and Conference Center in Bellagio, Italy in 2002 (Moodley & Adam, 2004). Moodley is a coauthor of a publication that resulted from a consensus panel I chaired, *Democracy and Diversity: Principles and Concepts for Educating Citizens in a Global Age* (Banks et al., 2005), which was a follow-up to the Bellagio, Italy conference. She also wrote a paper for the conference on global migration and citizenship education that I organized and chaired that was held in Seattle, Washington in 2015 (Moodley, 2017).

This book epitomizes Moodley's first-rate scholarship, intellectual gifts, and commitment to social justice, racial equality, and cosmopolitanism. It merits a warm reception and far-reaching influence.

James A. Banks

REFERENCES

Banks, J. A. (2004). Multicultural education: Historical development, dimensions, and practice. In J. A. Banks & C. A. M. Banks (Eds.), *Handbook of research on multicultural education* (2nd ed., pp. 3–29). Jossey-Bass.

Banks, J. A. (2012). Multicultural education: Dimensions of. In J. A. Banks (Ed). *Encyclopedia of diversity in education* (vol. 3, pp. 1538–1547). Sage Publications.

Banks, J. A., Banks, C. A. M., Hahn, C., Merryfield, M., Moodley, K. A. . . . Parker, W. C. (2005). *Democracy and diversity: Principles and concepts for educating citizens in a global age.* University of Washington, Center for Multicultural Education.

Bethune, M. M. (1952, April 24). My last will and testament. Daytona Beach Florida: Bethune-Cookman University. https://www.cookman.edu/about_bcu/history/lastwill_testament.html

Castles, S. (2017). The challenge of international migration in the 21st century. In J. A. Banks (Ed.), *Citizenship education and global migration: Implications for theory, research, and teaching* (pp. 3–21). American Educational Research Association.

Charity Hudley, A. H., & Mallinson, C. (2011). *Understanding language variation in U. S. schools.* Teachers College Press.

Conchas, G. Q., & Vigil, J. D. (2012). *Streetsmart schoolsmart: Urban poverty and the education of adolescent boys.* Teachers College Press.

Cookson, P. W. Jr. (2013). *Class rules: Exposing inequality in American high schools.* Teachers College Press.

Gándara, P. & Hopkins, M. (Eds.). (2010). *Forbidden language: English language learners and restrictive language policies.* Teachers College Press.

Gorski, P. C. (2018). *Reaching and teaching students in poverty: Strategies for erasing the opportunity* gap (2nd ed.). Teachers College Press.

Gray, R. (2017, August 15). Trumps defends White-nationalist protesters: 'Some very fine people on both sides.' *The Atlantic.* https://www.theatlantic.com/politics/archive/2017/08/trump-defends-white-nationalist-protesters-some-very-fine-people-on-both-sides/537012/

Howard, G. (2016). *We can't teach what we don't know: White teachers, multiracial schools* (3rd ed.). Teachers College Press.

Lee, C. D. (2007). *Culture, literacy, and learning: Taking bloom in the midst of the whirlwind.* Teachers College Press.

Leonardo, Z. (2013). *Race frameworks: A multicultural theory of racism and education.* Teachers College Press.

Lustgarten, A. (2020, July 26). The great climate migration. *The New York Times Magazine.* https://www.nytimes.com/interactive/2020/07/23/magazine/climate-migration.html

Mahiri, J. (2017). *Deconstructing race: Multicultural education beyond the color-bind.* Teachers College Press.

Mayo, C. (2014). *LGBTQ youth and education: Policies and practices.* Teachers College Press.

Moodley, K. (2017). Citizenship, identity, and human rights in South Africa: Viewed through the lens of xenophobia. In J. A. Banks (Ed.), Citizenship education and global migration: Implications for theory, research, and teaching (pp. 107–129). American Educational Research Association.

Moodley, K. A. & Adam, H. (2004). Citizenship education and political literacy in South Africa. In J. A. Banks (Ed.), *Diversity and citizenship education: Global perspective* (pp. 159–183). Jossey-Bass.

Sensoy, Ö., & DiAngelo, R. (2017). *Is everyone really equal? An introduction to key concepts social justice education* (2nd ed.). Teachers College Press.

Solórzano, D. G. & Huber, L. P. (2020). *Using critical race theory in education to recognize and respond to everyday racism.* Teachers College Press.

United Nations, Department of Economic and Social Affairs, Population Division, *International Migration* (2019a, September). https://www.un.org/development/desa/en/news/population/international-migrant-stock-2019.html

United Nations, Department of Economic and Social Affairs, Population Division. (2019b). *World population prospects 2019 Highlights.* https://population.un.org/wpp/Publications/Files/WPP2019_Highlights.pdf

Valdés, G. (2001). *Learning and not learning English: Latino students in American schools.* Teachers College Press.

Valdés, G., Capitelli, S., & Alvarez, L. (2011). *Latino children learning English: Steps in the journey.* Teachers College Press.

Preface

Race and politics figure prominently in this book. Having spent the first third of my life in apartheid South Africa and having taught at a "tribal" university explains this focus. Legalized race classifications determined one's life chances from birth to death. My autobiography reflects on this fate and how ordinary folks dealt with it. Historically, this narration is located in the apartheid era, prior to the release of Mandela and the negotiated settlement.

My story blends descriptions of details with academic interpretations. This mixture of narratives differs from the usual abstract academic texts. The reader, hopefully, gains more insights from what is in part a memoir, and in other parts educational lessons drawn from numerous micro-experiences. The subjects range from indentured labor to expropriation, from a comparison of Gandhi and Mandela to the subsequent corruption of his party, from anti-Semitism in Europe to welfare colonialism in Canada, from sectarianism in the Middle East to strategies for combatting bigotry in America.

Culture also features prominently in this story and is normally used in a positive sense. People having strong traditions, rituals, literature, and rules for social engagement are envied and admired. An in-between minority of Indians, isolated through residential segregation, transformed marginalization into cultural cohesion and collective solidarity. Ethnic socialization strengthens self-worth in the absence of recognition. At the same time, through turning inward, there is always a danger of social isolation from other excluded groups in the country. Culture can also be used for the opposite goal of manipulation. The South African state fostered different cultural traditions for divide-and-rule purposes. Setting up racialized, "tribal" universities, even on the basis of linguistic differences among Blacks, for example, restricted intergroup contacts between students. The state defined from above essentialized notions of group cultures: Blacks were better suited for studying agriculture; Indians with a perceived "ancient culture" were assumed to possess a more philosophical bend. Science education was excluded or a low priority.

Critical reflections on culture are also necessary because imposed identities are never monolithic. Internal splits between Hindus and Muslims, between half a dozen Indian language groups, between secularists and religious dogmatists have to be navigated at all times. When I dated a Hindi-speaking fellow student outside my Tamil language group, it was seen as almost a serious violation of a cultural tradition among rural members of my extended family. The chauvinistic glorification of narrow definitions of culture can become a straitjacket of conformity pressure that stifles individual imagination.

My education occurred in the context of the overall English colonial dominance in Natal. Uninformed teachers in this tradition completely disregarded our historical background in high school. In my class, Ela, the granddaughter of Gandhi, was not once asked, "What was your grandfather like? What do you remember of him?" This cultural imperialism has now fueled an ongoing revolt at South African universities, as happened in the United States, where Black students demand recognition of readings by Black authors and Black history.

My repeated academic journeys allowed me a comparative view on global ethnic problems: Germany, especially Berlin; the United States at Yale University in New Haven, Connecticut; Egypt in chaotic and lively Cairo; and finally settling in officially multicultural Vancouver on the west coast of Canada. The varied experiences taught me some sober lessons about ethnic strife, which I discuss in Chapter 11.

Acknowledgments

In getting started on this work, two people played a significant role. First is James Banks, with whom I have worked over many decades and who throughout my career has been supportive. On one occasion he asked me a question about my life in South Africa, which he may have regretted as he listened to a long monologue in reply. But at the end of it he suggested that I consider publishing the story and pointed out Sonia Nieto's autobiography as a form that I would find of interest. The second person is the late Pierre van den Berghe, my first sociology lecturer in Durban, South Africa, who became a close friend when he moved to Seattle. For years, he encouraged me to isolate myself for a few weeks to write about my South African childhood and educational encounters at the tribal college.

Similarly, I have learned so much from our two daughters, Kanya and Maya, who both had radical suggestions for turning things around to avoid the stodginess of academic writing. Their helpful edits and technical know-how were always just a phone call away. Engagement in my project has added new heights to our relationship as they urged me to tell more. Even my now 105-year-old mother, when she once heard I was working on a book, reminded me of something she had learned from a woman writer in India: "Always keep a little flashlight beside your bed, paper and pencil, so that when you have an idea at night, you will not forget it the next day!"

My sisters, Devi and Subithra, in South Africa and my brother, Sundru, in Denver are great at recounting the past, though our versions often differ considerably. For the liveliness of their imaginations, the fun and laughter, I am thankful. From my brother-in-law, Mahmoud Rajab, I always glean valuable information about community strategizing in times past.

To Rhona and Harvey W. Weinstein, Maria Tippett, and Sudeshnie Naidoo, I am grateful for their astute comments on a first draft. These were most helpful in its reshaping. I am appreciative of my longtime schoolfriend Ela Gandhi for taking the time to drive me out to revisit the Phoenix Settlement near Durban where her grandfather, Mahatma Gandhi, had set up the first self-sufficient community. Despite the valiant attempts at reconstruction, it was sad to see the effects of the destruction that had spoiled this once beautiful space. It was heart wrenching to learn that typesetting pieces from Gandhi's press had been sold as scrap metal by looters.

Many friends and colleagues in Cape Town have encouraged me to write from a more personal perspective: Marilyn and Richard Honikman, Jenny Boraine, Jane Slabbert, Wilmot James, Jane Raphaely, Kate Owen, Lucia Thesen, and the late Mike Savage. Breyten Breytenbach, whose mellifluous use of language and refreshing perspectives mesmerizes audiences, took the trouble to provide me with examples of work in a similar genre to the one I was hoping to pursue. I valued the lively dinners spiced with political discussions with Anincka Classens and Geoff Budlender.

At Yale, in the Southern Africa Research Program, I got to know Hermann Giliomee and learned much from his provocative questions and arguments. We have remained good friends over the decades since then.

Several stalwarts of the struggle—the late Alex Boraine, the late Van Zyl Slabbert, Mary Burton, Fatima and Ismail Meer, and treason trialist Norman Levy have taught me much. From the charismatic Van Zyl, I remember the warmth of his friendship over many visits to the bush and his Bokkies cottage. Few friends could be as open, honest, and realistic about sharing real-life concerns, hopes, and fears for the future of South Africa as we mused in front of the fireplace. When we coauthored *Comrades in Business* (Adam et al.,1997)*,* his ability to cut through jargon with humor will never be forgotten. From Alex, his quiet and powerful diplomacy in the development of the Truth and Reconciliation Initiative is memorable, as is our friendship over the years. From Mary, her role in the Black Sash has been an impressive model of modest tenacity of purpose and she is inspiring for her lived principles. I could always rely on good arguments also from Solly Benatar and Andre duToit.

From the distant past, a friendship lasted to this day with Jairam Reddy and the then U.S. Consul, John Savage in Durban who defied official restrictions by providing rare opportunities for socializing across race lines in his open home. Njabulo Ndebele's multilayered, writing one can ponder endlessly. I feel fortunate to have spent time with him as cofellows at STIAS in Stellenbosch, and to remain in friendly contact over the years.

Above all, I owe a huge intellectual debt to my heart's partner, Heribert Adam. When writing in a new genre compared with our traditional academic writing, and exposing such personal material, one often experiences self-doubt about the wisdom of the project. Heribert has supported me throughout—emotionally, intellectually, and in every possible way. He has been there for me, commenting critically, taking over the trivia of daily living, and encouraging me to keep on writing. During the COVID-19 pandemic, I could not have dreamed of being sequestered with a better partner on Pender Island, though by the end of this work, he may not feel the same.

Lastly, I acknowledge that the academic parts of this memoir draw upon my previous six books, numerous chapters, and journal articles. Some passages derived from earlier work, mostly in Chapter 11, are expanded versions, all with the permission in contracts of previous publishers.

Introduction

I grew up in South Africa under apartheid. Durban, my hometown, is the subtropical holiday capital on the east coast famous for its attractive long sandy beach with windswept tall palm trees and an amusement park between the roaring ocean waves and a row of high-rise hotels. During my youth this beach was divided into four sections: one for Blacks, one for Coloreds (mixed-race people), one for Indians, and a broad stretch of the best swimming beach for Whites, near the shopping center and aquarium. Only the White section had shark nets installed, not the narrower Indian, Black, or Colored sections. Maybe that was the reason I never learned to swim. Ironically, the entire beach is located on the Indian Ocean.

The partitioning of beaches was one bizarre facet of apartheid, superficially described as total racial segregation. But Indian ice-cream sellers, White lifeguards, and Black nannies attending to White babies mingled happily along the entire row. Yet if they wanted to swim, sit on a bench, eat in restaurants, visit cinemas, try on clothes in stores, or use the public toilets, they had to conform to their race classification. This system of legalized racism dictated from birth to death one's life chances solely on the basis of race. Where one was born, which hospitals one could use, which schools children could attend, allocation of differential funding for education determining the quality of education available, where one could live—all were determined by the color of one's skin.

This book is my story as a South African sociologist of Indian ancestry. It describes how a marginalized community of cultural hybrids—Indians on African soil—lived with, fought, and braved the bewildering racial engineering under apartheid domination and subsequently as inauthentic outsiders and eternal foreigners under Black domination. I convey my experiences of living, studying, and teaching "race," ethnicity, identity, nationalism, and critical multiculturalism in five countries on three continents: South Africa, United States, Germany, Egypt, and Canada. Using an autobiographical lens, I have attempted to connect the personal with the cultural and political. By sketching the different political landscapes, my aim is to further a more global political literacy.

In an enduring relationship with a supportive academic husband of German origin, we have raised two independent professional daughters: Kanya, a political scientist with a D. Phil. from Oxford, and Maya, a medical doctor on the faculty at Stanford. I grew up, as the eldest of four siblings each succeeding in their chosen field: sister Devi, a perceptive psychologist and popular columnist in Durban;

sister Subithra, an innovative South African businesswoman and coordinator of an American student exchange program; and brother Sundru, a creative entrepreneur in the dental field, and a longtime resident in the United States. Together with their spouses, this extended family spans Hindus, Muslims, Jews, and Catholics.

Due to limited economic resources and educational access, my parents had no opportunity to obtain a secondary education, let alone university credentials, though it ranked highest in their aspirations for us. In terms of emotional wealth and wisdom, however, they were extremely rich. They were both ordinary and extraordinary folk. Their ancestors arrived as immigrants and indentured laborers. Initially, they were welcomed in the 1860s as a source of "reliable" labor, under a system of indenture. When they chose the option of a small piece of land in lieu of return passage, they were subsequently resented. The Wragg Commission of 1887 reported that "the majority of White colonists were strongly opposed to the presence of the free Indian as a rival and competitor, either in agriculture or commercial pursuits." Neglected in this view is the fact that many indentured laborers, who chose not to repatriate, lacked agricultural know-how. Some even sought employment in municipal maintenance work, sometimes as street cleaners, living in barracks provided by the municipality. In different ways they endured restrictive legislation and slipped through the nooks and crannies of apartheid to ignore its scars, never to hate, but fill the cracks with their own ingenuity to make the best of what was available.

My father's behavior broke every stereotype of chauvinist Indian men. At a time when the celebration of a first child's arrival was reserved for the birth of a son and the birth of a girl child was greeted with muffled congratulations or "Never mind, the next one will be a boy!" my parents went to great lengths to celebrate my arrival. A special gold necklace with a lotus leaf on which Sarasvati, the goddess of learning, is seated, engraved with my name and birthdate on the back, and a gilt-edged invitation printed to celebrate the event, remain as reminders.

My mother told me that the necklace was made by an Indian woman jeweller, a rarity in those days. With these beginnings, I now understand how the world was open to me. Nothing could crush me, neither apartheid nor gender bias. I had the feeling I could achieve anything I wanted. My father gave me the courage to pursue aspirations without fear of failure. My mother sustained and reinforced this throughout my life by believing in me. Despite her traditional outward appearance, she left no tradition unquestioned and was always willing to change when supported by sound reason. She was farsighted enough to steer me toward sports, photography, and painting, away from the customary focus on domestic skills for girls. Together my parents paved my way to be self-assured and never afraid to try.

Whether this experience is typical of a heterogeneous Indian minority of barely 3% of the total South African population, is only one aspect explored in this book. If one looks comparatively at statistics of educational performance, social mobility, saving rates, divorce, crime, and other indicators of a "good life," one almost has to answer in the affirmative. But this simplistic portrayal of self-made success ignores different degrees of discrimination and oppression of other less fortunate communities. Individual agency is but one factor of the complex puzzle of why some people are able to break through barriers and others not. It is far more difficult, if not altogether impossible, to distinguish what can be attributed to cultural traditions, collective habits ingrained over long times, or reactions to an oppressive order.

Through this autobiography, I hope to convey what can be learned, both academically and personally, from this journey, which spans several decades. The lessons are mostly implicit rather than direct "how-to" advice. I seek to sketch a nuanced understanding of how racism has unfolded differently in each context. I aim at conveying a deeper understanding of discrimination and inequality through storytelling, framing these within my life's journey as a woman with multiple, yet coherent, identities.

If there is a message and political vision I would want to foster, it is to defend interconnectedness and cosmopolitanism. That does not imply abandoning a local community. Affinity to a local space does not have to be parochialism. Even patriotism does not have to be "the last refuge of the scoundrel." Critical patriotism, or "constitutional patriotism" (Habermas, 1998), can be a legitimate source of pride and national cohesion. From progressive nationalism, which includes robust criticism of the in-group, flows solidarity with fellow citizens and residents. In contrast, aggressive nationalism, the blind, uncritical glorification of the in-group, leads to supremacist habits. In short, it is political literacy that my story tries to illuminate.

I focus on how subordinate minorities not only live with, but overcome formal and informal discrimination. In apartheid South Africa they responded to their disenfranchisement individually and collectively, some in alliances with other politically excluded groups, the Black majority, and the so-called Coloreds. Some dropped out into private concerns, while others, for the most part, emphasized education for upward mobility. Given the size of the group, a significant number became activists of different persuasions and methods as supporters of liberation movements. What determined this range of responses and differential outcomes? Was it parental pressure and community-initiated reactions? Was it the teachers, cultural traditions, or public role models? The tyrannical environment of racial restrictions produced some of the world's most inspiring leaders, like Gandhi and Mandela, whose legacies guide us even after their deaths.

As a graduate student in the United States. I was exposed to the civil rights struggle of African Americans and the life of Martin Luther King. The discrepancy between the American promise of equality for all and the reality for people of color became obvious. African American patience and the spirit of resistance moved me. In the subsequent phase of my journey to postwar Germany, the reaction to the Holocaust vacillated between reexamining anti-Semitism to memorializing victims in what was called *Aufarbeitung der Vergangenheit* ("grappling with the past"). Emigrating to an officially multicultural Canada made me into a "visible minority." Indigenous groups ("First Nations") mainly used the legal system to challenge and embarrass the liberal state to live up to its broken promise of equal treatment. In the Middle East, sectarianism disguised deep class cleavages.

In conclusion, my comparative study transcends the usual focus on racialized minorities as victims. Instead it highlights the power of agency even under unfavorable conditions. Indians, like many other minorities, made their space utilizing the power of communal mobilization at the expense of individual aggrandisement. In his book *Native Nostalgia*, the perceptive Black South African author Jacob Dlamini (2009) shows "that the world of apartheid was not simply Black and White, with resisters on the one hand and oppressors on the other. It was a world of moral ambivalence and ambiguity in which some people could be both resisters and collaborators at the same time" (p. 156). I explore further how my family and I were both victims and beneficiaries of this gray zone in the middle of a racial hierarchy.

At the same time, the comparative parts of this memoir aim at drawing lessons from the complexity of racism and its multiple specificities in other divided societies. Implicit in this approach lies political literacy that educators and activists can develop according to the varied social contexts they encounter. How different communities elsewhere engage in supporting, accommodating, and resisting imposed status hierarchies, inspires innovative strategies and counteracts ethnocentrism. Integrating my deeply personal experiences may enhance reader engagement while adding authenticity and credibility to this work.

CHAPTER 1

Expropriation and Dislocation

One beautiful summer day in 1961, I had just returned home from university. My classes ended early on that day. I was enjoying a cup of tea with our neighbor, the lawyer Reggie Ngcobo, who lived down the road and had dropped by to ask if my father had time to join a doubles tennis match on the weekend. Although he was a prominent successful lawyer, he was forced to live in the domestic living quarters at the back of a Colored family's home on the street, because Black South Africans were not allowed to own property in the city. After a while, there was a knock on the front door. Three White men in formal dark suits and hats asked to come in to serve a notice to us. Immediately, I thought they had come because of our Black neighbor, who was, strictly speaking, living illegally in the city albeit at the back of someone's house. Was it because interracial social contact was frowned upon? My mind raced to the thought that there was nothing illegal in this social contact. It did not even involve any alcohol: It was unlawful under apartheid to offer alcohol to a "person of color," but we were both "persons of color." I ushered them in. They looked critically at Reggie, sitting confidently and comfortably on the sofa with a cup of tea in his hand. After all, in the custom of White South Africans, Indians and Blacks were meant to be serving, not be served as social equals. I did not offer them a seat. They stood at the door with a sheet of paper, an eviction order, informing us that we had to vacate our own freehold home. They drew my attention to the stipulation that the house was to be fumigated at our own cost prior to vacating. These, they pointed out, were the regulations under the Group Areas Act. They offered this information deadpan, expressionless and unfeeling. I was fuming. They needed us to sign that we had received this notice. Sensing the seriousness of the situation, Reggie offered to leave. I asked him to stay. Then I turned to these bearers of bad news and said: "How do you feel about doing this job? Do you know what it means to be forced to leave your own home because of some racist government planning? Do you think this is fair?" They looked down to avoid my gaze. Then I exercised the only other source of power left to me. "I will not sign this now. You will have to come back after my father has seen and read this." They left, expressionless, without another word. I wondered what Reggie was thinking—that he couldn't even have a chance to be evicted because he was never allowed to own a place in the city to begin with, though he could well have bought several houses? This moment brought home to me, yet again, my relative privilege as an Indian South African, a member of a middle ethnic group. I too, despite our indentured ancestral roots, was a beneficiary of a racially ranked apartheid society.

The house on Heswall Road in Durban was an English-style three-bedroom brick bungalow with a galvanized metal roof through which we could hear the rain pattering down. At the back of the house was a separate bedroom, shower, and toilet intended for "the help."

In South Africa, regardless of one's economic status, there was always someone with less, available to serve as household help. Almost everyone lived with trained incapacity to operate without "help," either paid or from family members. In front of the house was a small garden with pink, green, and red hollyhocks that grew beautifully tall against the warmth of the white stuccoed brick walls. There was a generous, covered veranda. At each corner, lush flowering bright-red bougainvilleas trailed down wooden trellises. On warm summer evenings we gathered here, cooled by the evening breeze for extended after-dinner conversations.

In this home, three generations dwelled. Our family of four children grew up there. It was where my youngest sister was born. My grandfather, who lived with us until his 93rd year before passing away, took his afternoon nap on the veranda in a canvas lounging chair, where he read the *Reader's Digest* and travel books. Each day around midafternoon he watered the plants before his daily walk to the pub for his evening glass of whiskey and conversations. Visiting pubs was stigmatized in the Indian community, but Grandfather convinced my parents that he enjoyed listening to other people's stories of what was going on. That Indians were not allowed to purchase alcohol without a permit worked in his favor, so he needed no excuse to have his daily libation at the pub.

Every year we held special prayers to honor Sarasvati, the Goddess of the Arts and Learning, who was called on to bless our books and pray that we would be successful in our educational pursuits. Many Divali celebrations honoring the Goddess Luxmi to bless the home with prosperity took place in the living room, accompanied by the classical chants of Tamil music by Subbulakshmi. Little clay lamps were lit around the ledge of the veranda every evening of the festive holiday. This space was also the site for gatherings to spill out into smaller groups. It was there, on my 18th birthday, that a major argument about whether South Africa was a fascist state or not took place, threatening to end the party. Two otherwise activist antiapartheid liberals, sociologist Margo Russell and her husband Martin, argued it wasn't, using finer theoretical points about aspects of fascism to defend their positions. Most of the others thought of the term *fascist* as being synonymous with *racist*, interpreting the argument as unsympathetic to our plight under apartheid. They felt insulted to even question the comparison, such was the nature of polarized arguments at the time.

Despite the limited size of the house itself, we were able to accommodate an out-of-town student, Dane Naidoo, for a year. He was studying for a teacher's diploma. He slept on a bed at the back of the house in the closed-in porch area. The following year, my parents responded to a call from a student organization at the University of Natal's "Non-European" section to assist in providing accommodation to African students affected by the curfew laws. Under this law, Africans were subject to arrest if found on the streets after 9 p.m. Such laws made it difficult for African students to use the library after work and get back home in time. The student who came to us for a few weeks before exams was Ambrose Ndungane, then a law student. Our home became a lively and interesting place. Cousins from out of town, who needed support with their studies and could not afford to stay in the city, also spent school nights in town with us occasionally. The mind boggles, in retrospect, about how even small spaces could expand with such generosity. Every alcove could become a place for a small improvised bed to sleep on. We were not alone in this. Many Indian families did the same. This is something we would never do today unless the customary appropriate space of a separate bedroom and bath were available for the guest. Sharing, as opposed to rigid rules about individual space, enabled these accommodations to take place. The Indian kitchen always provided for unexpected guests with ease. I never recall sending people away without something to eat.

The White, Colored, and few Indian neighbors on this street comprised a harmonious community. It was not difficult to see the inverse economic status of neighbors compared to the wider society. The best-educated and probably the wealthiest was the Black lawyer who rented quarters at the back of a house but parked his two high-end cars on the street in front. Next were the few wealthy, but less educated, Indians who owned their homes. Two working-class Colored and White neighbors were the poorest financially and educationally and lived in rented White-owned properties. Mr. Mistry, the owner of the duplex next door, was a boxing trainer and discretely ran a boxing school in a building behind his home frequented by a few young Africans. On the upper floor lived the Mistry family. Mrs. Mistry never left the house. All the shopping for food and even clothing was taken care of by her husband. She was expected to conform to his dietary preferences as a "pure" vegetarian and prepared the most delicious dishes. On occasion, the grapevine had it that her relatives smuggled some cooked meat under a pile of rice and vegetables, to provide a change for her. But despite this confined existence, she had a vivid imagination. Using a "peeping Tom" lens from one window to the next to survive the isolation, she constructed the most amazing stories about the goings-on outside. Whether they were based in fact or not, their value for us lay in the humor they brought us. The lower floor of this duplex was rented by a well-known Indian photographer, Dennis Bughwan, and his talented, attractive wife, Devi, who was a high school teacher at the time. She went on to become Professor of Speech and Drama at University College. She was a pioneer in hosting the Sunday morning "Indian program" on SABC television, which she did in the most impeccable English, even anglicizing Indian names! She was awarded a scholarship to study at the Bristol School of Drama in the United Kingdom, and I have never forgotten her comment upon returning: "I felt I had been born there!"—so complete was her identification with her colonial education. Yet in earlier times, she had also familiarized me with alternative unrecognized highlights of the classics in Indian literature on law and justice. We were very close to them, and she was, in some ways, an admired, significant person during my adolescence. All in all, this was a congenial neighborhood, though there was little social interaction among the residents apart from exchanging ritualized pleasantries. Despite ethnocultural differences, neighbors passing by would stop to greet others who were sitting on the verandas on warm summer evenings, never failing to exchange a few pleasantries. One had the feeling we belonged in a community, very different from the government's ethnically exclusive notion of what constituted a community.

17 Heswall Road, the home from which we were being evicted, was located in the lower Berea area of Durban, a short walk to the Botanic Gardens and a 10-minute drive to the beachfront. With a 2-minute walk up to Botanic Gardens Rd, we could take a double-decker bus to go downtown to the central shopping area of West Street. School was within a 15-minute walking distance. It was the first home my parents considered themselves fortunate enough to have bought, having heard about the previous Indian owner's intent to sell. They were able to secure an informal purchase.

Properties such as this were not easily accessible for purchase by Indians like us, because of a British colonial gentleman's agreement made with conservative Indian politicians. They promised to save face for the British colonial government that we would self-police ourselves. The agreement was for Indians not to make offers on White properties listed for sale, self-censor and stay out of such desirable areas. One has to realize that there was no easy, open real estate market for Indians at the time. We were dissuaded even before the Group Areas Act from purchasing property in the central urban areas. Many who do not understand the context cannot imagine that this is not simply selling your old home and shopping to buy another. Because of the prejudice and discrimination that Indians faced in renting accommodation, the first priority was always to own one's home rather than rent. My parents had saved every penny to make this purchase. Our consumption patterns were conservative and restrained. We never went out to restaurants. Apartheid made that easy since we could not eat at Whites-only restaurants, and there was one shabby café-type restaurant, Goodwill Lounge, frequented by Non-Whites. Regardless, at the time, it was not part of the culture to eat out commercially anyway. Our family policy was to save as much as we could and never to purchase any items unless they could be paid for in full. In so doing, they avoided the temptations of "buy now, pay later" and the trap of massive interest payments. Many people joined community-run, interest-free thrift clubs. One that I knew of comprised 10 trustworthy families, each contracting to contribute 10 pounds a month, and each, in turn, was promised to receive the total of 100 pounds in succession. It operated on trust so that once one received the entire amount one didn't bail out but continued to contribute so that others could receive the same when their turn came.

To ensure that there would always be money in the home, it was a symbolic cultural practice in Hindu homes to keep a brass container near the prayer lamp in which an amount of money was always kept for emergencies. There was a sacredness about saving and growing money. One could borrow from the container, but it should always be reimbursed with the addition of some extra funds. This was the closest we came to developing at once a puritan as well as a capitalist habit, circumventing the profits of White-owned banks. The home was blessed if it had funds and all the more so if it met the obligation of sharing.

It seemed ironic, indeed, that the men who delivered the notice came from the Department of Community Development to move us out of our established homes into separate ethnic enclaves. In actual fact, they were engaging in community destruction through racialized social engineering. Eventually, after several extensions to the deadline, the house was fumigated and sold below market price to a newly arrived British immigrant. The fumigation requirement added insult to injury. It felt as if we were to eradicate our vermin-like presence before it could be occupied by White people.

The new English immigrant who had purchased the home walked into the house without customary greetings. Later, without asking for permission, he began using our telephone, until my mother rose to her full height of 5 feet 4 inches and said, "You have no right to enter our home until we move out and you take possession. And even less of a right to use our phone without asking, so please leave!" He took his revenge later. My mother had had a special rose planted in a pot on the veranda that she had started from a clipping and took it with her when they vacated the house. He insisted that the potted plant belonged in the house and had to be returned. The purchaser already had all the attributes of quickly acquired racial arrogance and expressions of entitlement toward us lesser beings of color. How easy it was for a White immigrant to become a member of the ruling class, regardless of their class background, simply upon setting foot on South African soil!

Of all the injustices of apartheid, the displacement of people from the homes in which they lived for decades left indelible memories of powerlessness. In the grand scheme, the Nationalist government justified segregation as promoting greater group harmony and avoiding intergroup conflict. In reality, there was never any conflict when individuals of different groups lived together as they did on our street.

The trauma of displacement we all felt is hard to describe. A poignant case was that of an uncle who cultivated a few acres of land as a skillful vegetable and fruit gardener in Sea View on the outskirts of Durban. For years, he grafted special fruit trees in a beautifully tended orchard surrounding his home. He supplied a steady stream of friendly neighbors, both White and Black, with high-quality produce. He was greatly respected. He had to walk away from the land he had tilled and fertilized, leaving behind all the fruit trees and plants he had so lovingly cultivated over the years. Forced to live in an apartment while waiting to find land to build another home, he never recovered and died within a year. Strangely enough, these wounds never leave a person. Some 40 years later, I was on a plane from Cape Town to Durban and I began a conversation with the White man beside me. I asked where he lived in Durban. When his response was "Sea View," I felt a lump in my throat. I ended the conversation there. After all those years, I still harbored a resentment. This man, who now probably lived on land my uncle had farmed and from which he was expelled, was no doubt unaware of the tears shed on the land he now occupied.

It wasn't as if one could look at other available real estate and find a new home easily. Because of the scarcity of property designated for Indian occupancy in the few enclaves near the city, prices were highly inflated for dwellings not even closely resembling what we were forced to leave behind. Land available for Indian occupation was located miles out of town. We were urban people who had lived in the city, not far from amenities. White Jewish friends, incensed by this legislation, offered to purchase the house to allow us to continue living in it, but it would have been illegal for Indians to live there, even after it had been sold to a White person. Recognizing that it was time to move on, my father declined gratefully and put his energies into seeking an alternative place. As always, my father felt the need to be positive, find smooth transitions, and cause as little anger and disruption as possible to the family. For a few years, they moved into an apartment while seeking a suitable place.

The next level of emasculation came when my father had to go to the Department of Community Development, which was offering displaced Indians coveted alternative building sites for sale on the outskirts of the city. Despite being located 10 miles out of town, potential buyers had to almost grovel to purchase these. My otherwise confident father became deferent and almost submissive in the presence of the controlling, authoritarian, arrogant young man who had the power to open up available land. He insisted on showing us the worst sites possible. When Heribert, then a visiting German academic who was to become my fiance, offered to go with my father the next time to see what was really available, the reception at the same housing office changed radically. In the presence of a White friend, new and better options came forth as now being available. How humbling it must have been for my father to be "rescued" in the land of his birth by a young White foreigner. Scenes like this entrenched the powerlessness of my parents' generation, though they downplayed it to save face with and for the rest of us.

We, the younger generation, were irritated by what seemed to us a passive response to this legislation. We engaged in protests to express our opposition. Only decades later, as my father lay on his deathbed, did these issues surface in his hallucinations. He seemed to be panicking about "not having a place to stay. We are six people, we can't stay in such a small place . . . the government took my home, they forced me to close my business . . . and no one ever apologized to me!" A few hours later that day, as his condition worsened, he insisted that we call the manager of the now racially integrated beachfront apartment to which they had downsized in 1994. When she arrived, he asked her, in his weakened state, "Can we stay on here? Are we allowed to stay on here?" This rather gentle English woman had tears in her eyes. "But Mr. Moodley, you can stay here as long as you like. You own this apartment." And then he seemed at peace: "Thank you! Thank you!" At the age of 86, he was still the provider of secure accommodation for his family. Remnants of the trauma of displacement still surfaced. Yet he had stubbornly refused to apply for compensation for land confiscation, provided under postapartheid legislation, as his children had urged him to do. "There are masses of poor people in this country, whose needs are greater and the new government has to attend to that, so we will forego our claim," he replied. At one level, he had moved on.

This quality of hiding the shame of powerlessness had followed me all my life as I observed the way my father and his peers were treated by White men regardless of their standing in life. Visits to doctors' offices meant sitting in the non-European section of the waiting room to see the same doctor. Once my father was explaining to the doctor what my condition was in the only terms he knew when he was rudely stopped for using terms which prejudged what the ailment was. I felt hurt to see my father humiliated in the presence of his child. Apartheid had bestowed on White professionals the incredible gift of "effortless superiority." I admired the quiet resilience of men of color whose superiority shone through a deep understanding of the shallowness of such shows of arrogance and the illegitimacy of its basis. For the most part, they never internalized this denigration.

My father sometimes humored us with stories about the way his White office mates ridiculed him for offering his daughters a university education. "They're going to land up with the pots in the kitchen anyway, so why waste your money on educating them?" They talked about Indians breeding like rabbits . . . whose women smelled of spice and never wore perfume. I now know why, when I was 16, my father gave me among my gift of books, a bottle of Chanel No. 5. These comments about "breeding" affected one of my father's Indian colleagues so badly that when his wife had a third and fourth child, his colleague hid this "embarrassing" information from his superiors. From then on, at each office Christmas party only two gifts were prepared for this colleague's first two children, since officially, the others did not exist!

I write this memoir as a person who was allowed to vote for the national parliament in the country of my birth for the first time only after I had turned 50, and whose parents and grandparents had never been allowed to vote in their entire lifetimes. I could have voted 10 years earlier for a newly created but segregated ethnic parliament that excluded African participation. However, my community largely boycotted this sham institution of a "tricameral parliament" with just over 20% participation in the election. My esteemed brother-in-law, Mahmoud Rajab, even ran as a successful candidate with the rationale that he wanted to undermine the obnoxious system from within. For others like myself, the fact that Africans were excluded from having a vote and Mandela was still in prison outweighed the vague possibility of what we saw as co-optive and divisive reform.

The other so-called middleman minority, wedged between the Black majority (78%) and the dominant Whites were the Coloreds. At the beginning of apartheid in 1948, Whites constituted 20%, but have now declined to less than 9% of the population, because of emigration and a much higher birthrate of Africans. In this official racial hierarchy Blacks, Indians, and Coloreds were all classified as "Non-Whites." A different history, culture, differential rights, and settlement pattern characterized each of these three disenfranchised groups. This heterogeneity facilitated the apartheid design of divide and rule. Ironically, the apartheid race classifications are still in force informally in everyday life and formally in contested legal affirmative action policies.

Our colleague and friend, the Ugandan sociologist Mahmood Mamdani (1996), pointed out that apartheid attempted to "racialize" Whites by unifying English and Afrikaans speakers and people of other European backgrounds, but to "ethnicize" Non-Whites by reinforcing their linguistic and cultural divisions. Yet Whites, initially called "Europeans," are culturally the most diverse group, with their most relevant cleavage running between Afrikaans (60%) and English speakers (40%). In the bitter Anglo-Boer war at the turn of the 19th century, the defeated rural Afrikaners lost about 10% of their population as well as political control of their two republics. English dominance of the economy was consolidated with the discovery of gold and diamonds.

While most Indian South Africans live in KwaZulu-Natal on the east coast of Africa, about 90% of people classified as Coloreds live in the Western Cape. They speak Afrikaans and belong to Calvinist churches. To all intents and purposes, they could be considered brown Afrikaners, despite not being accepted socially by White Afrikaners. The Cape was also declared a "Colored labor preference area," giving this group preferential employment rights over Blacks. Unlike Blacks, Coloreds and Indians did not have to carry passes to prove that they were legally in White urban areas. Apartheid nationalists, despite their shared linguistic heritages, abolished the qualified franchise of Coloreds in the Cape and Transvaal, because the majority of Coloreds would have voted for the English Liberal party after World War II.

Most South Africans, particularly Blacks, are multilingual nowadays. South Africa now recognizes 11 languages as official, among which Zulu and Xhosa are the most common, but English nonetheless became the lingua franca. Despite all the close contact, Whites (with a few exceptions of those raised on farms), Coloreds, and Indians have never really learned any African language except for the most minimal communication. This says something about the status of languages: We learn only what we consider valuable. Then defying the usual ability to pick up languages we hear in use around us, there is a trained incapacity to learn what we do not deem worthwhile knowing.

The apartheid setup tried to keep the majority of Blacks out of the cities and concentrated in the desolate rural areas. Only the economically useful were allowed to live in urban areas under "Section 10 Rights." Black women who were employed as domestic workers had to live in women's hostels if no accommodation was provided by the employer. Where such accommodation was available, they were never allowed to cohabit with their husbands. Police with dogs, regularly patrolled domestic quarters of homes to check for undocumented men. "Influx control" was used to enforce such regulations. In practice, that meant that "illegal" shacks in the Black townships surrounding the cities were regularly demolished and their inhabitants "endorsed out" into Bantustans as illegal "surplus labor." Blacks were expected to administer their own poverty and police themselves in the Bantustans. This saved employers and the state from carrying the social costs for education and old age care. It also destroyed the traditional Black family structures when the migrant labor system recruited men for work in the gold mines for 9 months, but did not allow their family members to join them. Expropriation and dislocation of Indians at least kept the nuclear family together. The enforced migrant labor system for Blacks damaged Black family life irreparably in addition to disrupting the traditional peasant culture in the rural areas.

CHAPTER 2

Relatives, Parents, and Customs

MY MOTHER'S STORY

My mother, Amartham Moodley, was born and lived until her late teens on Point Road (now renamed Mahatma Gandhi Road) in Durban in the extended family home of her eldest cousin, whom she considered her brother. Uncle KP, as he was called, was the manager of the African compound nearby. The house was one of the benefits of his job, as was a ration of staple food. It was a rambling, corrugated metal bungalow, with a large veranda, overlooking the harbor. From there, one could see the ships come and go. One side of the house had another large separate room with an old-fashioned bathtub, hand basins, and toilet facilities. The other side had a nice garden. It was always a little dry and windswept so it seemed that not much survived in the garden except a hardy lawn. Food preparation for celebratory gatherings of the extended family took place there in large pots on open fires. The entire joint family was accommodated here. My mother's mother died there, at age 22, after giving birth to her third child. From what I could gather it sounded like a form of placenta previa from which she bled to death, while the family tried in vain to use traditional methods to cure her. My mother's father then took care of the three children, two boys and a girl, supported by the larger extended family. Apparently my maternal grandfather would cook their meals and leave this ready for them when they came home from school. He had immigrated to South Africa as a young man from Vellore in India, though in her late 90s my mother mentioned that he really came from what was then known as Ceylon, but didn't want other Indians to know that. He hadn't completed secondary schooling but said they were much better educated in British colonial Ceylon, compared to India. He played the violin, she said, and often wrote and recited poetry for them. Each month he received subscriptions to newspapers from India from which he would read to the family after dinner. From what we could tell, he arrived as an indentured immigrant in the early 1900s, eventually finding work as a porter at a major hotel on the Durban beachfront. He could not have earned much, but when he died, about six years after his wife passed away, he left an insurance policy of 20 pounds each for his three children. He had also purchased a grave plot where his young wife was buried and left a small bank account with some savings for the family to care for the children. My mother said that he had accumulated savings from the tips he obtained as a porter and from taking on additional work.

After my grandfather's death, my mother's aunt took on full responsibility for the three then-orphaned children. Together with her own five children they bonded as a family of brothers and sisters with no distinction being made as to which children were "hers" or not. Never was the term "cousin" used to differentiate them. To all of them, she was Amma ("mother"), and they were sisters and brothers. No mention was made about the additional cost of caring for three extra children. Though they might have used the capital my mother and her brothers inherited for investments, the initial capital was returned to the three siblings upon each of their marriages, to start their own new family lives. In those days, the 20 pounds that they had each inherited was a substantial amount. Sharing characterized the ethos of family morality. It was considered their duty to take care of each other without mentioning financial costs. If they struggled, they were all in it together. Family honor was a driving force. My mother mentioned that after her father died, her aunt contacted his relatives in India to inform them. The relatives in India responded that she should send the three children with all the funds left for them and they would care for them. Once she heard the importance of "all the funds," she had serious doubts about their motivation. She tore up the letter. That effectively ended any information about those relatives.

My mother's second eldest cousin, Uncle KR, took on leadership of the family. He moved away from the house on Point Road with his newlywed wife, his mother, my mother and her two siblings to the city to a more upscale brick-and-tile bungalow on North Street. Why Grandmother did not remain with the eldest son, as was customary, but moved with the second son is unclear. The only explanation could be that Grandmother now had to take care of three orphaned children and Uncle KR and his wife already had five children. The new house, one of few available for Indians to purchase, was located fairly close to the racecourse. This was where I happened to be born. In those days when a woman was to have her first child, she went back to her maternal home, where she could be taken care of in a manner to which she was accustomed and transition into motherhood. Prior to the segregation this had been a mixed neighborhood. Across the road lived Afrikaans-speaking Mrs. van der Merwe, whose husband worked on the railways. She was our dressmaker. She turned beautiful silks, taffetas, and Broderie Anglais into fabulous dresses for us. I recall the smell of her heavy smoking and congested chest coughs. They were known as "poor Whites" who rented accommodation. Other Indian, White, and Colored families, with whom we were not in frequent contact, also lived on the street.

148 North Street is firmly etched in my mind. It came to life all the more when I took my husband to see it years later. All that was left of it was a flattened piece of earth—no houses on the block were left. Instead there were squatters living in tents with barrels to collect water occupying the entire block. All the Indian residents, living in nice bungalows that they owned, had been forcibly evicted simply to fit the grand design of apartheid to complete racial segregation. To this day, the land where their now demolished homes once stood stands barren and unused.

Uncle KR's home had been the main center of the extended family since it included my grandmother. The family gathered for celebrations of festivals and for dinners before and after life cycle events: the birth of new babies, weddings, engagements, and funerals. Many a crying bride bid farewell here to her family as she departed to the home of her newlywed husband. Then there was Divali, the festival of lights, with much feasting, albeit vegetarian! Special sweets were prepared, beautifully arranged on silver doily-lined platters and offered to all the neighbors regardless of their religious backgrounds. As the sun set, children were taken to a room full of fireworks, from which we could choose and go out to light up the sky together. Each child received money from every uncle, blessed by Grandmother, symbolizing a wish for their prosperity. Newlywed brothers and their wives lived in this home for a short while after their marriages to become socialized into the family's ways.

Uncle KR and his brothers were very meticulous people and perfectionists in whatever they did. When you entered the front door, one was reminded of an English drawing room. From the little contact they had with White people they were able to imitate some colonial lifestyles without being stigmatized by members of their own group. The sofas upholstered in warmish dark green or maroon velvet, Persian area rugs, and French brocade curtains made for an impressive entry. On the wall to the far side of the room was a large Victorian-style, unsmiling portrait of my grandmother. I often wondered where her husband was, as there was no picture of him. An impressive-looking grandfather clock chimed beautifully on the hour. There were also framed photographs of the first, now vintage model, car they owned, with my uncle in a stern unsmiling pose, standing proudly beside, dressed in an English tailored suit with a colonial khaki helmet. On another wall was a photograph of all the brothers looking on, while a contract was being signed with the Shell company for the purchase of a garage, their second collective business acquisition. In the middle was my grandmother, seated at the table, immaculately dressed in her pastel silk sari. Her presence had symbolic value: It held out the promise of religious blessing for the enterprise. Two beautiful Cloisonné vases and a few brass pieces were positioned on stiffly starched, off-white, hand-crocheted doilies on gleaming oak chests of drawers and side tables with barley-twist legs. A few nice bookcases with leaded-glass, art deco–style doors lined one wall as one entered, containing leather-bound books of Indian classics and the Encyclopaedia Britannica, more for decorative purposes than for daily use since the bookcase was always locked. I am reminded of a comment by my father who was an avid reader. He could never be without a book or newspaper whenever we visited relatives and was bored with endless trivial conversations. He once said to me, shaking his head, "Look at this house—books are ornaments. There are no books here that people read every day. There are no newspapers, no magazines!"

Uncle KR was the patriarch of the family; even though he was not the eldest son, he took on responsibility for all the siblings and their children. He had great business acumen and commanded respect. With pooled labor resources, the family first bought a store they called Crystal Cafe. It was immaculately outfitted. Art deco–style biscuit cases contained stacked packets of Baker's Marie Biscuits, Tennis Biscuits, Eet Sum Mor Biscuits, and Boudoir Biscuits. Sparkling glass containers with shiny lids held different candies, like domino-shaped licorice of all sorts, smarties and jelly beans in lustrous colors, and twisted barley stick candies. Decorative large metal cash registers, with old typewriter-type keys, stood prominently on the marble counters, ready to take cash payments with a loud ring each time the drawers were either open or closed.

At the store, the windows and mirrors gleamed from constant cleaning. To the side was a milk bar, creating delicious milkshakes made in a large stainless steel container with a whizzing rod in the middle that made the milk and ice cream foam. After school I sometimes took my friends there and as a treat enjoyed these wonderful milkshakes and cream-soda floats.

My mother's family grew up with a sense of plenty, though we knew they were not enormously wealthy. They were rich in the way they behaved and in the high regard in which they were held in the community. They had style and class and had slowly risen from indentured status without losing their own traditional roots.

From the small plot of land that the previous generation was given in lieu of the cost of passage back to India, my mother's aunt and her husband established a cane farm. Later, upon the death of her husband, she farmed vegetables for the family's use. The sons worked at different jobs during holidays. Some assisted at a large bakery, others worked as cleaners in the boiler room of ships, or painted ships' decks being repaired in the dry dock. They gradually pooled resources and grew their finances. From her contact with a few White families my mother's aunt learned about their style of cooking, selectively including these in the family cuisine. Roast chicken with stuffing, Madeira loaf cakes, and scones were incorporated as regular treats for dinner or tea. Their lifestyle ascent seemed authentic because it was gradual and selective and they never lost the sense of their own roots and identity. Assimilation it was not, but integration of features they considered worthwhile gradually revealed adoption of changing aesthetics.

The store was run by my mother's brothers, of her then combined family, before they were married. Bearing in mind the larger picture of the greater good of the family, they worked for a minimal personal salary, board and lodgings included. My mother once told me that the brothers took turns sleeping on matrasses on the store floor at night to be there early to open the store. Their one main meal, prepared by the women in the family, was always in the family home on North Street. Gradually, they accumulated enough money to purchase a garage and, much later, a block of apartments in which each brother could have his own space and which would cost less than separate individual homes. After work, my father, as the new son-in-law in the family, contributed his accounting skills, managing the family finances. For this he was offered one of the apartments in this new building of nine apartments, called Crystal Court.

9 Crystal Court on Lorne St. was my first home when at primary school. We lived in the apartment on the ground floor, and upstairs lived all the other uncles and their families. There were always cousins to play with after school and aunts to visit. The presence of stay-at-home mothers and aunts made a huge difference to our visits with cousins at any time. The doors were always open. There were

goodies to eat, and we always felt welcomed. On the uppermost floor was a large roof garden used to hang out clothing to dry, with enough space for us to run around and ride bicycles, or hold large family parties on weekends.

Uncle KR then studied very carefully everything he could learn about making ice cream. This addressed a market niche in Durban at the time. What began as a small ice cream manufacturing project was located on the ground floor of the apartment block. Despite Uncle KR's lack of formal education, never even having completed primary school because he had to go out to earn enough to support his widowed mother and younger brothers, his economic savvy was remarkable. He learned from scratch how to make ice cream and became a pioneer in the field. Gleaming stainless steel appliances stood on spotless steel tables. A machine containing soft ice cream was fed through a nozzle into endless blue and white lined lightly waxed paper cups, shifting along a moving band and then sealed each mechanically with a thin cardboard lid, to be immediately refrigerated. Several bicycles with refrigerated containers filled with dry ice were used for small deliveries. Gradually, a fleet of three delivery vans was acquired to expand the business called Crystal Ice Cream. Once the business flourished, he later sold it to a much larger English company called Wall's Ice Cream.

Whatever he undertook, Uncle KR perfected. In retrospect, what they achieved with so little formal education amazes one.

I recall the scene at his home as he engaged in the simple task of hedge clipping. With the aid of the inevitable gardening help, in true South African style, he clipped using a ball of string and a weight to get a perfectly straight hedge. In the middle encircling the gate, the hedge took a semicircular form, always precisely maintaining proportion to the rest of the hedge. In those days, bougainvillea was not used for the beauty of its colored flowers, but was kept trimmed to maximize the hardy green leaves and keep it from flowering. He learned how to arrange flowers from a European woman, and how to make salads unknown in Indian cuisine: potato salad with boiled eggs and a mayonnaise dressing, tomato salad where the tomatoes were cut into little cubes and then marinated with chopped onion in a vinaigrette dressing.

Travelling to India, he came back with trunk-loads of gifts for the whole family—shopping on an unprecedented scale—musical instruments for children, brass lamps for the local Hindu temple, saris for all the sisters-in-law, Indian champals (sandals) in all sizes for the children of eight siblings and glass bangles for everyone. In the days when all this had to be shopped for in different places in India and transported onto a ship, the mind boggles at what this must have taken to accomplish. Clearly, there was a huge philanthropic urge that drove the concern for a larger whole than one's own individual family.

My mother's aunt, who had become her "mother," whom we considered to be our grandmother, was a very Victorian-looking woman. She wore her hair combed tightly back into a well-pinned knot. No hair was out of place. She only wore plain pastel-colored crepe de chine saris, which she always meticulously ironed herself. Her blouses were called "chemises" and had button-down fronts and long sleeves with lace at the edges. She wore black patent leather Barker anatomical shoes with a very low heel and a strap buckled across. Her large stud earrings were set with red garnets in a circular form. This cacophony of blended cultural styles told a story of its own. Only very occasionally did I see her smile. I never saw her laugh. Her life had been very difficult. Her own father had died when she was very young and her widowed mother (my great-grandmother) remarried a man who was not very well disposed to this stepchild. She was married off, she said, "to a much older man" before she had even reached the age of puberty. I wondered: How could a mother allow this to happen to her child? Did the mother have no power to object? How old the man was with whom they arranged the marriage we never really knew, because together they had four sons and a daughter and my mother's aunt said he had been very kind to her. In effect, she was the half-sister of my mother's own mother Thanjamma, though only the term "sister" was always used, never stepsister or half-sister.

Adults were responsible for all children in the family. School lunches were sent daily from the café, delivered by bicycle from the ice cream factory, for the entire family, not just the nuclear family. When after-school home language teaching was found to be of a poor quality, a Tamil tutor from India was hired for the entire extended family. This meant that after school we all descended, about ten of us, on the home in North Street. First we would be served scones or biscuits and tea, and then we had the classes for a few hours daily. Admittedly we were a distracted lot who made the teacher's life miserable. Our internalized devaluation of this home language, together with an unimaginative pedagogic style of an "uncool teacher," made us willing failures. Minority children all too quickly learn the differential value of home languages and learn to use it only minimally when speaking to grandparents.

The family's gradual adaptation to Western ways was undertaken without becoming submerged in the individualism that accompanied assimilation to Western living. However, the resistance slowly grew as each brother married and their wives each demanded more for what their husbands were contributing to the workplace. The unquestioned acceptance of the authority of the older brother over the younger ones declined and very gradually eroded the consensus of the earlier conforming unquestioned acquiescence of the premarital joint family.

One story has been repeatedly told about my youngest Uncle Vadi's new bride, Auntie Radha, who joined the family and like all the others spent the first few months in the family home. She had come from a very rarified background in Pietermaritzburg. They were taught well and only spoke the most classical Tamil and a very cultivated English. At the same time her one brother, despite being a London-trained barrister from Lincoln's Inn, ensured that she had a Victorian upbringing, shielding her from reading even Jane Austen for fear of exposing her to the romances they contained. Their home, I recall, had a beautiful grand piano, tall dark antique Dutch cupboards, filled with bone china crockery. Despite having all the trappings of a Westernized decor, it was far from a liberated environment. The name of her family home, engraved on one of the stone pillars supporting the large gates leading into a long driveway lined with gum trees, was ironically SWARAJ, which meant freedom from colonial rule.

One day, the new bride, now in the home of her in-laws, thought it would be a great idea to go for a walk from the house to the café where her newlywed husband worked. Without mentioning this to the other women in the family, she planned to surprise him. It involved about a 20-minute walk. But to her surprise her husband, though initially happy to see her, said she should go back quickly as her presence in the business place would be frowned upon by the others. Shocked and distressed by this, she returned home, only to face the disbelief of the other women in the family for what she had done and to be given the cold shoulder by the eldest brother-in-law for the rest of the week. So, after some days, she went up to him and in her most eloquent Tamil, said something to the effect that "I, small as I am, in your esteemed presence, ask for forgiveness for what I have done." By then she had figured out that the women never left the house to go to the male public domain of "the business." His unyielding answer was that he would not forgive her! This seemed to be the other side of the generous patriarchal caring that characterized all the other inclusive moves in family building.

Other family stories reiterated a similar assertion of patriarchal power. When Uncle KR's daughter, whom he had sent to Teacher Training College, fell in love with a fellow student and after a few years wished to marry him, he was irate. Marrying a "mere teacher" was completely unacceptable. Point-blank refusal for a few more years continued when her boyfriend's family came to ask for the hand of his daughter in marriage to their son. One day, the daughter picked up enough courage to leave the home without permission. A formal Hindu marriage ceremony with the cooperation of the groom's family had been arranged in secret. For years the family mourned as if she had died. In a similar situation, her elder brother had fallen in love with a girl who had helped one of my aunts care for her children after school. Since she became defined as "servant class" and was considered to have a darker complexion to boot, this union too was rejected, another marriage was conducted without parental approval. For many years this dissension in the family discolored all the harmony of preceding times. Everyone became drawn into the conflict for their purported collusion in one way or another. But with the passage of time, the birth of grandchildren smoothed over the cracks and the situation normalized. The patriarch even apologized decades later. When this once-rejected couple had a daughter, my uncle told me that this child was so beautiful, she would one day marry a doctor. I recall standing up to him, even though I was just a teenager, and saying laughingly, "Don't you think it would be better if she became the doctor herself?" By then he had softened enough to comment about me to my mother, "She's a very clever girl!"

Strangely enough, this very patriarch softened over 2 decades when I was about to cross racial boundaries and marry a German. Two factors made a difference in his change. Firstly, I believe, though my mother never really admitted it, that to get him on my side, she sought his "help" in this "difficult" situation she was facing, of my "out-marriage." Also, in this case, he assured her that she shouldn't worry because the German doctor was at the same level of education as I was and the Germans were a traditional "cultured" people. He reminded her of the early work that German writers like Max Muller had done on Indian civilization. Similar interchanges emerged when a few years later, my sister's relationship with a Muslim lawyer came up. In this case, he assured my mother that he knew the family well, that they were a very traditional family, and culturally they were of the same class as us. In fact, he thought they had earlier been good Hindus like us. In both cases class, tradition, and education trumped out-marriage, which would earlier have been unthinkable.

MY FATHER'S STORY

My father's trajectory differed very much from that of my mother's family. Absent was the joint family business acumen of my mother's family, though my father's family supported one another in need. The siblings pursued different ways of earning a living and carving out lifestyles for themselves. Hence there were marked differences in the economic standing of the brothers and sisters.

My paternal grandfather, an only child, immigrated alone to South Africa as a young man. His parents had previously migrated from India to Mauritius, an island off the southeast coast of Africa, when he was a child. They ran a small store in a place called Flaq. They must have gone with the intention of returning to India. Since they did not trust the banks, they put their daily earnings into cans and buried them in the ground under the house for use when they were ready to return to India. They also stored gold sovereigns, which they had brought with them. Shortly before they were to leave, they opened up what was to be their savings and found that ants had burrowed into the corroded cans and had eaten away some of the notes. In great distress, they went to the bank to show what had happened. The bank was surprisingly sympathetic and gave them some currency based on the notes that were still salvageable, albeit damaged. So they cut their losses and returned to India.

In India, my grandfather found some of his father's activities, such as cock fighting with his friends, quite repulsive. Soon after his mother passed away, he saw no reason to stay on, and took off on the next ship heading to Mombasa in Kenya on the east coast of Africa. When on board, he befriended a few people who convinced him that he should stay on and join them in Natal, a province on the east coast of South Africa. He did this. Upon arrival at the docks in Durban, recruitment agents were ready to take people to work for them. He must have looked good because someone offered him a job as a supervisor of labor at the railways. This was his first job. He was able to speak French, which he had learned in Mauritius, as well as Tamil, Telugu, Hindi, and Kannada, which impressed them as well. The way in which ethnicity, language, and identity featured in his life were informative about people and migration at the time. His family religion was Hindu, and their home language was Kannada, though the parents had lived in several parts of India, such as Hyderabad, which had a large Muslim population and where other languages were in use such as Telugu, Urdu, and Hindi. He must also have added Tamil to his languages there. What I found of interest was that he was given a surname of Moodley when he arrived at the Durban port of South Africa. His name was Ramiah, but English officials needed a surname, and I assume they simply added "Moodley," which was an abbreviated form for *Mudaliar,* a title originally used in Ceylon for a class of individuals loyal to the British crown, and arbitrarily given to some lacking a surname. At the time, identities were fluid; people added names given to them without challenge. Such was the nature of powerless immigrants, just content to get "their papers" approved. Identity was situationally constructed.

When my grandfather began work on the railways, he must have had a reassuring presence. One of his White supervisors took him under his wing and introduced him to an attractive single Hindi-speaking woman called Phuljhari. Though his linguistic background differed from hers and most Indian marriages were linguistically endogamous, this didn't pose a problem for either of them. They began a life together and had three children, but this life as a couple was short-lived as she took ill while the children were very young. Some members of the family say she died after a snakebite. The youngest daughter was only 4 years old and the two older boys, who were at school, were asked to come home as she wanted to see them. My grandfather told the story of how she asked him to bring the family prayer lamp, some water in a ritual brass container, leaves of a sacred plant called Tulsi, and a prayer book. The lamp was lit and she took the children's hands and placed them in his. In the presence of the sacred lamp he had to promise that he would take these children back to India with him to his village, marry a woman from his community, and bring her back to take care of him and the children. My grandfather did as he was told. I once asked him how he managed to travel alone with three small children. He told me that when he had to go to the bathroom on the ship, he tied the children to the mast of the ship so that they would not fall overboard! To this day I cannot imagine how he could have afforded all this travel even though they most likely travelled as deck passengers on a sailing ship.

Upon arrival in India, he took them to his ancestral family. After a while, the family introduced him to a young widow called Govindamma, who had one son. Deeply entrenched taboos in Indian society relegated widows to an outcast status. Her parents were keen to give her a new chance in life, so they sent her off with their blessings and offered to take care of the one child she had from her previous marriage. My grandfather, having been raised in colonial Mauritius, thought nothing of remarrying a widow. To him it seemed only fair. This young woman, who was to become my grandmother, never overcame her reluctance to leave India and go to the dark continent of Africa. She was by caste a Brahmin and vegetarian, and for as long as I remember she never forgave my grandfather for bringing her into a situation where she had to mingle with meat-eating people with different customs! What was interesting is how unconventional my grandfather had been, crossing linguistic barriers in marrying his first wife whose language was Hindi. Throughout his life he added languages without ever identifying himself as belonging to one group only, as was the case for most others. Ethnic, linguistic, and caste differences played different roles among the Indian immigrants to South Africa.

Grandfather must have loved his first wife dearly, as I recall that each year, despite his remarriage, he went to a special temple in Isipingo, near Durban, and after a short silent moment before a lit prayer lamp, he released a white dove in her memory. Nevertheless, he had a long life in South Africa with his second wife, who raised three children by his first wife and from the second marriage had five children, three sons and two daughters. My father, Percy Mariemuthoo Ramiah Moodley, was the first born in South Africa of my grandfather's second wife. His given name was Mariemuthoo, though in the family he was affectionately called Chinnap, meaning "little fellow," because he already had two elder brothers and a sister from his father's first marriage. The name Percy was one he was given when he went to work for an auto parts company in the city of Durban, where he began as an all-round clerk and assistant at age 15, when his father pulled him out of school to go to work. My father was proud of the name Percy and preferred it to his given name. He never suffered from a loss of his identity. He had gone to the local school for Indian children and wrote with pride in the school's centenary publication that his first school was in a grass hut.

My paternal grandfather seems to have "retired" rather early and sent his older sons off to work to bring in funds, while he built his house and took charge of its maintenance on his savings. The house was a large rambling, wood-framed house with a corrugated metal roof in an area called Clairwood on Horsham Road. It had a covered Victorian-style veranda and was very basically furnished with a few old pieces of furniture: an antique hall stand on which to hang men's hats, a large dining table, and a few upholstered chairs. Large wood-framed pictures were tacked on the wall. My memory of it was that it had a large garden with mango and guava trees. Under the large guava tree was the small temple he built for my grandmother's daily worship. Beyond that, at the very back of the garden were the ablution facilities where there were drop toilets, or outhouses. In the outlying residential areas where Indians lived, unlike the White residential area, no sewer system had been installed.(My urbanized mother was horrified to learn that the municipality sent men each week to collect what they euphemistically called "night soil," dump it into a truck, and carry it away!)

For a few months my newlywed mother went to live there. As a city girl she was quite unaccustomed to this style of living, but she loved my father very much and respected his family so she never complained. "Never say we have nothing" had always been a guiding motto throughout her life. They spoke Telugu, and she was quick to mimic what they said and soon developed some working proficiency in the language, much to my father's amusement.

The family comprised one older half-brother, his wife, and children who had their own section of the house and a separate kitchen. Also together with my grandparents, in another section of the house, lived my father and his two unmarried brothers. His two younger sisters, who were taken out of school even earlier than the boys, had been married off very early. Strangely enough these two aunts who had taught themselves to read persisted in making the best of the little formal learning they had. They were both avid readers. One aunt went on to raise a family of five children who became a school principal, a magistrate and three lawyers, one of whom went on to law school for an LLD degree at Harvard, and subsequently became UN ambassador on human rights.

Although my father was forced to leave school at age 15 to go to work, he was so determined that he would make up for his lack of formal education that he took on extra jobs to earn more money so that he could afford part-time studies. After work he enrolled in evening classes at a technical college, studying bookkeeping and accounting. Once he completed his studies, "with Distinction," he was offered a part-time teaching position. As soon as he was able to get a driver's license, he offered his services to chauffeur his employer and his wife on excursions out in the country. He never spoke openly about what it must have been like staying over-night as a non-White person in segregated White hotels. So great was the desire to maintain images of being treated as equals in the eyes of the family, that these humiliations were most likely glossed over and the larger picture of having been in nice places superceded. As a boy from a traditional Indian home where it was not customary to use the full range of cutlery as in English table etiquette, he must have watched very carefully when they stopped over for meals. Now I understand why he was always teaching us, as kids, good English table manners. "This is how you place your cutlery when you've finished eating. This is how you distinguish the fish knife and fork from those for meat." And clear demonstration of how one piles food on to the upper part of the fork and spears peas, rather than the more sensible way to use the fork for scooping the food, American and European style. A full set of silver cutlery was bought and used with pride when we had guests, as part of this initiation process. It was always my father's responsibility to take and fetch from the laundry, the white damask tablecloth for formal dinners. Sometimes this led to awkwardness among our poorer relatives who were not accustomed to the use of elaborate cutlery and were used to eating with their fingertips, Indian style. Our practices were always modified depending on whom we were entertaining.

When I consider the choices my father made in his life, namely to improve his education, to engage in community work, and his selection of cricket and tennis as preferred sports, one understands one course of mobility. With some assistance from his older brothers, my father started a cricket club for youth in Clairwood. He also volunteered to work with the Red Cross, setting up a branch in his neighbor-hood. There he met an English health practitioner, Paul Sykes, who asked him if he could live with an Indian family to learn about their lifestyle in order to understand more about the prevalence of tuberculous in this community. My father facilitated this, and eventually Paul Sykes founded a clinic called FOSA (Friends of the Sick Association) to address the prevalence of tuberculosis in that community. At my father's funeral in 1998, a well-known lawyer and member of the tricameral parlia-ment, who had earlier worked as a clerk for FOSA, mentioned that throughout his life, my father never forgot his monthly donations to this foundation.

The choice of sports and, later, his business acumen, brought my father in contact with a largely professional peer group of doctors, businessmen, and law-yers. Since he was a very good tennis player, as evident in the number of tro-phies he had won over the years, his company was always sought. Later he played professionally, representing Natal in provincial tournaments. From these initial contacts, a number of the young doctors who had returned from their studies in London and Edinburgh initiated the idea of a family club, since as Indians we were excluded from existing clubs with tennis courts and other sports facilities. My father was invited to join with nine others in purchasing a large country house, which was converted into the Bellair Club. This was prior to the Group Areas Act, when it was still possible for Indians to own properties like this on the outskirts of the city. My memory of it is of a long winding driveway through broad-branched flowering jacaranda and flamboyant trees. Beautiful fragrant franjipani trees blossomed near the tennis courts. A short distance up from the courts, a large gazebo with a black slate tiled floor and octagonal wooden seats was located. From here we watched the games being played. The courts were of sand, which had to be rolled out with a large roller, and the lines freshly painted white. There were tennis lessons for the children too. I remember having tennis lessons once with Rod Laver, who visited the club for a day, though I didn't know just how famous he was until I was much older. The club was meant to make up for the social exclusion under apartheid. The clubhouse comprised a large wood-floored ballroom with a grand piano. Leading off it was a full-sized billiard room. The walls of this room had beautiful wood paneling, along which green felt-tipped pews were lined up. On the other side was a black slate board for recording scores in white chalk. The table was a rich, dark green felt, and the magic of the colored balls arranged in a triangle never ceased to excite me. We begged to be first to scatter the formation when the adults weren't playing.

One of the partners was Dr. Monty Naicker, who was "Uncle Monty" to us. He was a prominent political figure, serving as President of the Indian National Congress and later the South African Indian Congress. We looked up to him for his political courage. I remember when I was about 10 or 11 attending a mass meeting where he and Chief Albert Luthuli addressed the crowd. Afterward Uncle Monty led a small group of fellow protestors into a Whites-only waiting room at the railway station. They were all arrested. Then we drove his wife home. Some time later, he was one of the accused in the Treason Trial in 1956–1961, though released in 1958.

Many of the guests to the club were well-known politically involved people from across the racial spectrum. One figure that I recall visiting the club was author Alan Paton from the Liberal Party, who had written the beautiful book *Cry the Beloved Country,* later filmed in the Valley of a Thousand Hills, just 20 miles inland from Durban. On one occasion when someone offered me a small Grand Marnier to celebrate an event in the ballroom, Alan Paton, sensing my lack of familiarity with this drink, came over to me and gently advised me to sip it *verrry* slowly and swirl it around in my mouth before swallowing it!

Another visitor to the club was Dr. Yusuf Dadoo, a leading figure in the Congress-aligned Communist Party. A regular visitor was Dr. Goonam, a feisty, British-trained, politically outspoken Indian woman doctor who challenged Indian customary norms by smoking cigarettes in a long cigarette holder, while at the same time impressing the more conservative with her grasp of impeccable Tamil.

As we grew older the character of the club changed. My parents spoke, in hushed voices, about too much alcohol being consumed. Some of the partners were bringing women to the club without the knowledge of their wives. After a while, we no longer went there as a family, though the men continued with their billiards and tennis on Saturday afternoons, often well into the evenings. At around the age of 55, when my father considered his tennis skills failing, he switched to golf, which he then played three times a week. Friends told me that he was very good, a "scratch" player, which I hadn't paid much attention to. The numerous trophies he won attested to this success on the golf course, but as children often do, we took this for granted or had little interest in our parents' activities and successes until it was too late.

When one looks at the lives of my forefathers, their arrival in South Africa, and the space they made for themselves, many lessons can be gleaned. With minimal formal education, they had few resources to challenge the conditions under which they worked and lived. The most they could do was to make the best of what they had. Racism and segregation did not feature as concerns they could take on. For sheer survival they relied on each other for support to get through day-to-day needs. Once they had families, children and siblings rallied together to build viable lives. How fortunate they were to be able to do this, unlike the destruction of family lives faced by Black South Africans with the removal of men to work on the mines away from their families. What chance did they have to provide children with the kind of cultural socialization that assumes intact family life? By contrast, despite the hardships of indentured life, Indian families were able to pool resources to provide children with what several American researchers (Coll et al., 1996; Huguley et al., 2019; Wang et al., 2020) cite as successful education for minorities through cultural socialization to contend with marginalization.

In the case of the early immigrants, they unknowingly engaged in cultural socialization organically. They had to share the little they had. There was minimal room for individual independence and freedom. Through these shared actions, such as joint families, sharing and related values, and respect for elders, a reference group was set up. Children were accountable. They had to contribute to the family economy; they had to listen to ritualized value-inculcating stories and legends. Reading and writing were considered sacred. Books were blessed. Education was the most valued goal for their children. The implications of these customary practices differed in their translation to economic success, even within the same culture. This is evident in the difference between the directions taken by my mother's family as compared to my father's family. The former mobilized joint endeavors, whereas the latter took more individual paths. Only later did the role of resistance to racial discrimination take place with the entry of the next generation of the formally educated, who could lead challenges against the government of the time.

CHAPTER 3

Experiences in Apartheid Education

ELEMENTARY SCHOOL

My elementary school education was at St. Anthony's School, an all-Indian, government-aided school, supported by the Catholic Church and run by Irish nuns. Most of the teachers were Indian women, some Catholic and a small number of Hindus. The school was run along English lines, with formal assemblies each morning addressed by the principal nun, Sister Dominic, after which each class walked in pairs to the sound of militarist march music, aimed at developing a positive spirit of togetherness and camaraderie among the students.

Each day when we entered the classroom, everyone stood up to say Catholic prayers, regardless of their family's religious persuasions. Our class was a multifaith one. There were Hindus, Muslims, Catholics, and Zoroastrians. We all wore school uniforms. No one ever complained about having to say the morning "Hail Mary" prayers. As my mother said to me, "When they pray, you say the same prayers. There's only one God and religions are like different streams leading to the same ocean." That stopped me from feeling alien. Without knowing it, my mother had resolved my emerging conflict about how I did or did not belong.

After assembly each day, while the Catholic Indian children recited their catechisms, we non-Catholics were being read chapters from the Old Testament by the somewhat prissy Hindu teacher, whose exaggerated clear diction I can still hear today. These stories captured my interest, except for the notion of heaven and hell, which seemed to arise from either the content or the teacher's discussion afterward. The Ten Commandments made me feel like I was often on the losing side of the scale, which featured in my nightmares. I had, in fact, committed more sins than good deeds. But one day, in my child's mind, I seem to have sorted it out. My reasoning went something like this: We are in a class with children from different religions and backgrounds; there is no way that whoever is judging us from up on high could know all about each of us and use one measure by which to judge us. I assuaged my own feelings of guilt with this thought, and the agony seemed to disappear. The other incident that made me question the motives of the nuns was when one of the nuns mentioned to us in our senior year what a good and worthwhile profession it is to become a nun. "All your needs are taken care of. You have a great place to live, your laundry is done for you, and you are always safe in the world." I remember thinking what a poor reason that would be for going into the solitude of a convent and leaving your family.

In retrospect, what strikes me most is the quality, commitment, and dedication that these teachers and nuns showed in their work as educators. Parents, regardless of their religious affiliations, entrusted their children to the school's care. Never was there an incident where Muslim or Hindu parents questioned whether their children were being indoctrinated into a religion different from their home beliefs. So great was their desire for education that they never questioned the content the children were learning and left curriculum issues to the professional competence of the educators to decide what was best. The other interesting thing about being in a government-aided all-Indian school is that I don't ever remember feeling like a second-class citizen in a racist society. The unintended consequence of racially segregated all-Indian schooling is that it seemed to shield us from any insults about our color or origins. Unarticulated collective solidarity left no space for the discriminatory political realities operating in the world outside.

My earliest memory of our undesirable presence was outside of schooling. It was when we visited the amusement park on the Durban waterfront. As young children we loved being taken there on hot summer evenings to ride the horses on the carousel, the Ferris wheel, the octopus and the whips, which twirled us around even faster at each corner, and experience the thrills of driving the dodgem cars. I wondered why we could never go for boat rides in the little pool area. My father always said the lines were too long to get in, when in fact it was only for White kids. But a time came when our visits to the waterfront amusement park ceased entirely. I overheard the adults talking about how Non-Whites were no longer allowed in all areas of the amusement park. Then I realized why when we went for evening drives on the beachfront, my father always took a different route so that we could no longer see the now inaccessible places we had enjoyed so much. I overheard the adults laughing at a friend's son, now a distinguished cardiologist in the United States, who covered his face in a white face cream called Hazeline Snow, and then said to his father, "Let's go to the amusement park now, I've got a white face and they will let me in!"

During my primary school years, the outbreak of African riots against Indians in 1949 was a terrifying experience. It took a long time for me to get over it. As an 8-year-old child, I still recall the taunts of *Shaya Makula!* ("Attack the Coolies!") that began suddenly one late afternoon when Africans marched with shields, knobkerries (clubs), and knives, shouting in unison to attack. Radios blared out that we should take cover and hide. We fled for our lives and hid in the darkened upper story of our apartment building from rioting mobs out to get at any Indian in sight. One of the African men who worked at the ice cream factory below, shut the doors to the building, and stood there to guard us and keep the building shut off. The sound of shattering glass came from all sides and it seemed only a matter of time before they would push the guard aside and break open the doors. I remember vividly being traumatized that my father hadn't come home from work.

My grandmother, who had just gone for a walk shortly before the attacks began, hadn't returned either. Both returned safely later that day. Our poorest relatives, however, living in wood and metal shanties in the outlying areas of Durban, were the worst hit, and many were hospitalized from injuries sustained.

One family's only source of income was a little convenience store, hyperbolically named Emporium Fruiterers in a passage called Madressa Arcade. The entire store was not much bigger than 50 square feet. Their main sales were from fruit sold individually, small cupcakes, and bottles of cold pop. Each morning the father went to the local market to buy boxes of fruit, and since he had no car, came back by rickshaw, manned by an African man in a tribal headdress. As can be imagined, the profit margin was extremely small and just barely supported the survival of the family of six. But they had "the dignity" of being self-employed in their "own business." Operating on such a small profit margin, many were the occasions on which they went "bankrupt" and the extended family bailed them out, giving them a fresh start. This was why it seemed so terribly unfair that rioting Africans broke into the store and beat up the father with a crowbar leaving him for dead. He had hidden two daughters in the toilet at the back of the store and was able to stagger there to open up the door before collapsing and being taken to hospital.

In the city center near where we lived, schools were transformed into refugee holding institutions for poor people escaping from the riots. I can still smell the disinfectant used to keep the place sanitized when we took relief supplies to the school. In a strange way, I remember thinking what fun it must be to sleep in rooms together with kids of the same age. I recall family discussions afterward, trying to make sense of it all. They commented that not all Africans were involved in the riots, that there were Africans who helped get my father and uncles safely home from work that day, after it became dark. Self-searching discussions in my extended family after the riots instilled in us the need to learn to speak "proper Zulu." We were not allowed to use the Tamil word *Kaapri*, a derivative from the Arabic term for "nonbeliever," to refer to Africans, but from now on we were told to use the word *Sudesi* which means the indigenous people of this land. A tree we had commonly called *Kaffir Boom* we were told to refer to as *Erythrina Kaffra*. Sheeting fabric known as *Kaffir Sheeting*, was to be called *K Sheeting*.

The riots against us left me with lasting fear of the possibility of our home being broken into. A paranoia about leaving dangerous instruments like chopping knives and crowbars around because they could be used to harm us remains with me today. On Pender Island in British Columbia where residents rarely lock their doors, I still hesitate when my husband asks me to go with him for a late evening walk on a trail in the woods. His calming admonition: "There is no Zulu behind the tree!" Recurring nightmares of an old disabled relative in a wheelchair being pushed off the cliff where they lived, and of young Indian girls being raped and brutally abused, which we heard happened in a number of homes, took ages to erase. It was all akin to postwar trauma, which took a while to put in perspective.

Another memory was riding the double-decker buses into town. We were never allowed to sit down below, and were told to go upstairs but were only allowed to sit in the last three rows at the back of the bus. As kids we never gave up harassing the White conductor about why we couldn't sit in front when the seats were unoccupied. And when we got off the bus and passed by the White boys high school on our way home, they yelled " black cockroach!" at us and we hurled back "white cockroach" in retaliation. In general, insults were bantered back and forth. We didn't experience it as deeply wounding and gave as good as we got.

My mother told a story about going to the butcher to buy meat. The White salesperson called out, "Mary, what would you like?" To which she replied, "John, I would like some lamb today." He indignantly responded, "My name isn't John!" And with a great sense of having beaten him at his own game, she retorted, "Really? Well, mine is not Mary either!" The background to the story is that all Indian women were called "Mary" by Whites, in just the same way that African domestic workers were given names like "John" or "Charlie" for men, and "Patience," "Beauty," and "Blessing," among others, for women. We simply refused to believe these derogatory labels as describing us and dismissed them as sheer stupidity.

When I was a young child, storytelling played an important role in family gatherings each evening, after dinner. In a multigenerational family, it was customary for one of the elders to tell stories, called *katha* in Tamil. My paternal grandfather, who lived with us, told the most engaging and gripping stories. He had a dramatic way to change his tone when he role-played what each character said in their own words. Sometimes the stories were in the form of a puzzle and we had to guess the outcome. Sometimes they were about a comic figure called Tenali Raman, the court jester, who tricked kings and rulers into recognizing the limits of their own judgments. Endless witty stories served as morality plays for ordinary people. That knowledge didn't only come from authority figures and power holders. Only recently did I discover the origin of these stories and how they related to our family history. My grandfather had a rich linguistic repertoire. Since the majority of Indians in Natal spoke Tamil, he extended his linguistic repertoire with Tamil and a very basic working knowledge of English. The stories he told us were narrated in Tamil since my mother was Tamil-speaking and our home language was Tamil. The stories of Tenali Raman I discovered much later were from Tenali Ramakrishna, a famous Telugu-speaking poet, scholar, and wise man from what is now the Andhra Pradesh region, who was a special adviser, and sometimes court jester, in the court of King Krishnadevaraya in the 1500s. Since my paternal great-grandparents came from Andhra Pradesh in India, my grandfather must have been steeped in these tales and legends, which he never forgot. Although the stories were in written form, many of the elders were unable to read complicated texts. They were accustomed to the oral tradition, which they continued.

On other occasions, a more serious theme from the *Bhagavad Gita* was featured regularly. The key idea was about an impending war between two families, the Pandavas and the Kauravas, who were cousins. Conflict arose when one family took ownership of the kingdom which was not rightfully theirs. Different factions supported each side, and many people were mobilized either for or against either side. And so, we were told about the discussion between two leaders, Krishna and his charioteer Arjuna. They each made an argument for and against war as a way to deal with this injustice. Krishna made the case that this was a just war and he had every right to engage in it. His duty was to seek a just solution. Arjuna, on the other hand, seeing the range of relatives and friends on either side, pointed out how many lives would be lost in such a battle simply for the sake of the kingdom. To engage in war with them would mean their involvement in killing people. He argued vociferously, would it not be the lesser of two evils to simply let them rule, eventually recognize the injustice, and inevitably concede without bloodshed? To save lives would be the better approach to take, he maintained, and laid down his arms. The theme would be embellished with quotes from the *Gita*, but to my embarrassment, I frequently fell asleep during storytelling. At the end, we were to say which side we would support and why. Who had the better argument?

Unfortunately, the pedagogic value of such an exercise, all too often, fell by the wayside. In my child's mind, these were old people telling boring stories about a time long ago, in a language we half understood and located in a place about which we knew little and cared even less. These stories had none of the appeal of fairy tales we were told in English school by teachers we held in higher esteem and in a language we valued more. Even stories from Greek mythology were simplified and had names that were familiar to us. They were considered valuable. The teacher understood and approved of them. The school had validated them. Not so with the Indian stories! I often wonder whether we would have listened better if our teacher had told similar stories reflecting us and included them as part of the school curriculum. Not only were Indian stories absent, so were African tales and history from the land of our birth.

On the other hand, I wonder in retrospect, why was I, around the age of 11 or 12, searching our bookshelves to look into some leather-covered volumes on *The Cultural Heritage of India*, by Radhakrishnan? Could I have been seeking who I was that I didn't see in what we were taught in school? The language in these volumes was much too difficult for me to understand. The philosophical terms mentioned made little sense to me, but I remember feeling that there was something of value there. Only years later did I see a connection and understand my own ambivalence about receiving alternate histories without any reference to stories we were being told.

As an adult, I came across the work of a Nobel laureate called Amartya Sen (2009), a Cambridge University scholar and Master of Trinity College, who wrote a fascinating book, *The Idea of Justice*. Building on the work of John Rawls, it deals with the role of public reason in making societies unjust. For the first time, I found a text that incorporated knowledge from different literary texts and drew upon the wisdom of many societies, including non-Western stories. In it, I discovered the very texts and stories my grandfather had been trying in vain to get us to think about. What impressed me most about Sen's text was its relaxed cosmopolitanism. It was not chauvinistic about any cultural contribution, but drew on the approaches that each society offered to the critical questions of our time, and indeed of all times. It also revealed in depth, familiarity about non-Western religions. The text bursts with insights and wisdom of a global nature and sought to offer a template for how to integrate multicultural insights seamlessly into our writing. In so doing, it avoids the pitfalls of disembodied cultural depictions so often laden with simplified stereotyped constructions. If we had been educated in this way, would we not be on our way to much better understandings of each other in a violent world?

SECONDARY SCHOOL

Durban Indian Girls' High was a respected secondary school. Our teachers were all either English, Irish, Scottish, or White South African. The ethos of the school was most definitely modeled along British public school lines. Our school uniforms were white dresses with navy buttons down the front and pleated skirts, two pleats on either side front and back, belted with a narrow navy belt. Navy blazers bore a badge with the school logo on the front pocket. The unstated expectation was that hair would be neatly braided. The subjects offered were English, Latin, mathematics or domestic science, history, geography, and biology. Physical education, art, debating, and music were taught but not as examinable courses. No science courses were offered in Indian and African schools.

In true policing style, a prefect system was in place. In my senior year, I was one of 10 prefects and wore a badge, pinned to my blazer. There was a head prefect as well, and our task was to make sure things ran smoothly at school. Among our tasks, we were to stand at the gate and note the names of latecomers, who were to be detained after school for being tardy; often they were punished by having to write 20–30 times the same sentence: "I will not be late."

What bell hooks (1996a, 1996b) said about being bused to White schools where she was taught by White teachers is true for our experience as well: the teachers were not interested in "transforming the minds of their pupils, but simply transferring irrelevant bodies of knowledge," which bore no relation to their lives. The White teachers' lives in apartheid South Africa were far removed from ours, given the institutionalized segregation under which we lived. How could they know our realities? Nor, in our view, did they seem to care. To be a professional teacher was to impart approved and stipulated knowledge to prepare us for their worlds of dominance. Even without being aware of it, we spoke like them, and we acted like them to do well in the school setting. I think it would be fair to say that all these teachers were ignorant and uninformed about the political situation in which they lived and how it affected us. In our class were some children who came from rural areas and spoke differently from us urban children. They obviously did their homework on the one table in their homes. Frequently they were made fun of when there were grease or curry spots on their exercise books, which the teachers encircled with a red pen. Why would it be any different? White teachers lived in completely separated areas. The public amenities they used were racially segregated. No social contact with "others" existed. The African cleaners who cared for their daily needs were "invisible," and the work they did to enable the good life for them was taken for granted. No ill will was consciously meant. It was the status quo and people unthinkingly and unquestioningly conformed. Miss Dorey, the very strict headmistress of Durban Indian Girls' High, ruled the roost with very high expectations of conformity to school norms and rules. The political inequity and injustices under which we lived and the different resources we had, played no part in her view of what made for good teaching relevant to our lives. The social distance that her imperialist manner and communication style introduced into every personal interaction with us as students or with our parents could hardly have been greater.

Everyone, including our parents, found the principal formidable, but respected the standards she had set for the school. Every teacher came well-prepared and on time. I will never forget how this headmistress took it upon herself to prepare us for the 10 days of home study that we were given prior to the highly stressful matriculation exams scheduled over 10 days. She outlined simple steps about setting goals for study each day: after every hour of hard studying, take a break of 10 minutes and go for a brief walk to get some fresh air or to get a snack. She encouraged us to keep very brief thumbnail notes on what we had studied for quick review, and be sure to get a good night's sleep. Contrary to my earlier assertions that she cared less, these were indeed examples of caring and communicating high expectations. They made us question assumptions that a dearth of personal warmth in communication is necessarily an indication of a lack of commitment to our success. And success meant mastery of dominance knowledge.

We grew up in an age without television. The radio, or wireless, as it was called, became our central source of information, other than books. On Wednesday evenings we listened excitedly to *Consider Your Verdict*, a program where court trials would be dramatized, suspects questioned, circumstantial evidence introduced, and then the thrill of "who was guilty?" and "consider your verdict!" In retrospect, it is unbelievable how much one could imagine without a pictorial image. We were creating the pictures in our minds, totally engaged! We were privileged in using our imaginations and listening skills rather than being glued to a screen with packaged images preempting our own constructions.

Radio was also used to belittle us, to make fun of our Indian accents and trivial chatter between two Indian men, in a program called *Applesamy and Naidoo*. For some time, we too laughed at this portrayal of ourselves, but there came a time when we became at first embarrassed, and later angry, prompting us to take action against the radio station for its racist, demeaning humor. Furthermore, the national SABC broadcasters had a trained incapacity to pronounce Non-White people's names. To look on this now in postapartheid South Africa, with political change this incapacity has disappeared! There is much to be written about the role of power and accents. Suddenly White announcers in the new South Africa have learned how to pronounce African and Indian names flawlessly, and African announcers switch codes with equal ease.

High school was a time of great politicization for me. During 1955 and 1956 the Special Branch (the security section of the South African Police during apartheid) conducted a series of raids on offices and private homes of hundreds of opponents of apartheid. All available evidence such as letters, papers, and pamphlets were seized in preparation for a show trial. Finally, on the morning of December 5, 1956, hundreds of policemen throughout the country invaded the homes of leaders of the Congress Alliance. 156 people were arrested—104 Africans, 23 Whites, 21 Indians, and 8 Coloreds—and charged with high treason, a capital offense in South Africa. People engaged in bus boycotts, pass burnings, and stayed away from work. In this ungovernable situation, the government declared a state of emergency. The Treason Trial was the main attack on the Freedom Charter. None of this was ever discussed at school. We lived disjointed lives, studying sanitized knowledge that had little to do with our everyday worlds. At the same time friends of our family were being arrested and placed under banning orders and house arrest for conspiring against the state, or seen as engaging in communist conspiracy. When we went to the temple for special prayers, the mothers and wives of those detained were praying quietly for their safe release.

Sometime later, after listening to many conversations in our home with Uncle Monty Naicker about their plight in raising funds for those charged with treason and the need for support for their defense, I approached the head mistress about raising funds from the students through several lunchtime sales. To this day I have an image of this slight but imperious white-haired woman. Her office had a dark glossy table covered with a plate of clear glass which was the common style at the time, apparently to protect the glossy furniture. I stood there after she allowed me in. I must have said, "Can I talk to you?" She immediately countered with, "Do you mean *may* I talk to you?" and then when I stood at one end of the table and put my hands on the table, she said, "Take your hands off the table!" All the time, she was meticulously peeling an apple and slicing it for her minimalist lunch, eating very carefully while she listened to my request to fundraise during lunch breaks in support of the Defense Fund. Her response was, "How can we support people who are enemies of the state?" To which I replied, "Well, they are innocent until proven guilty, and these funds are to support a fair trial, since they have been charged but not found guilty." In retrospect how right I was when those arrested were found not guilty and released. There must have been a weak spot of liberalness that I touched since she did allow me to go ahead. I must admit, I was shaking when I left her office. It had taken every ounce of courage to reply the way I had. After all, we had been so conditioned to follow authority that standing up to it alone was not easy.

Learning about state policies and legislation that affected the shaping of education for our future could only empower us as minority students, but school authorities failed to recognize its value. An example of this was the discussion around the Bantu Education Act aimed at relocating African educational institutions away from the cities into rural areas and ending earlier mission education, considered too liberal. As the Minister of Bantu Education expressed it in Parliament, "The basic principle of Bantu education is to keep the Bantu child a Bantu child. [They] must be so educated that they will want to remain essentially Bantu" (*Hansard*, 20,

17 June 1959, cols. 8318–8320). Conservatives justified this move as progressive, insofar as it recognized the distinctiveness of African culture and ways of life. The assumptions embedded ran deeper. Not only were Africans supposed to be biologically different but also culturally different. Deeply inherent were essentialist ideas about "African temperament" and "African mind," which justified the need for separate institutional arrangements. Crain Soudien (2015) summarizes how "cultural relativism became political pluralism." At the same time, one could hardly overlook attributions of inferiority to this specific African way of being. Here was an example of imposed ethnicity from above rather than people choosing to maintain their own identity. The goal was to isolate groups and regulate and inhibit access to wider opportunity. When people choose to self-identify from below and challenge the state's labeling, more genuine forms of identification and community cohesion arise from self-organization.

The Group Areas Act, which displaced settled populations, as well as the forced removal of thousands of Africans from townships such as Sophiatown, near Johannesburg, District Six in Cape Town, and Cato Manor near Durban, were all very much in our minds as students. We saw explicit images in the press, since this was prior to the introduction of television in South Africa, of brutal police removing some 60,000 Africans with no respect for their homes and belongings, and simply dumping them near Soweto. In this, all groups were unified. Students marched en masse in Durban with banners saying "Save our Homes." I recall how fearful my mother was when she saw me making the banner at home. She did not deter my participation. I knew where she and the community stood on our political participation and the danger of arrest. They believed firmly in "Education before liberation," meaning one should avoid arrest if it meant the closing of educational opportunity and danger to our lives. On the other hand, the implicit message of the African National Congress (ANC) was "liberation before education," which my parents disagreed with and even considered irresponsible. What I appreciated, in retrospect, was the autonomy they gave me to take a responsible stance without laying down the law.

High school had its liberating as well as disappointing moments for me. I was captain of the school debating team, which competed with other schools in the area. Overall, our school unequivocally triumphed in one debating competition after another throughout the province. To its credit, the school attempted to foster links with an African girls school, Inanda Seminary, which we visited for both sport and debating competition. This was a very happy time for us as we were very warmly received and made good friendships with peers we would never have had the chance to meet. We discovered we had more in common than we were conditioned to expect in our segregated lives. These would have been students with whom we could have continued contact in our future postsecondary education, were it not for the euphemistically called Extension of Education Bill being promulgated, requiring each group, henceforth, to attend its own ethnically separate universities. We were the last generation allowed to study together in the so-called open University of Natal, albeit in the non-European section.

In addition to captaining the debating team, I was chosen to represent the school at the Jan Hofmeyr Speech Contest, in which every high school participated. The preparation for this was quite telling. My English teacher in charge of preparing me told me that I spoke very well, but would have to work on the slight lisp that I had. So I went to the dentist to see what he would suggest to deal with this. Ignoring his recommendation for expensive orthodontic treatment, I continued to prepare the formal speech required. While my preparation focused on content and mainly on elocutionary aspects of the formal presentation, what was neglected in my preparatory training was the second part of the contest requiring an impromptu 5-minute presentation on a topic provided by the adjudicators. Having made it to the semifinals, I was given the impromptu topic, "Every dog has his day." I floundered badly. In typical colonial style, my prepared speech was flawless in content, articulation, and expression because it was so overrehearsed, but not so for the more spontaneous second part. I was deeply embarrassed by this failure. The two other candidates who went on to the finals were my cousin, Navi Pillay, who subsequently went on to become UN High Commissioner on Human Rights, and Iqbal Meer, who became an Advocate in London. Their performances were clearly better than mine.

My high school years involved taking photography lessons after school. My father enrolled me in a photography course with a well-known British portrait photographer, Norman Partington, so that I might broaden my interests. I learned some theory as well as hands-on developing and printing, which enabled me to set up my own darkroom at home. It was a great hobby and the Partingtons, who had a daughter my age, often invited me to their home over weekends. At first, I found their stilted conversations with very little substance, lots of word games and trivia, a little challenging. I had little to contribute. But a warmth developed between us, which made the contact easier over time.

I also engaged in some community work on the weekends. I'm not sure how it came to pass that I met a social worker named Violet Padyachee who worked at the Meyrick Bennett Child Guidance Centre. She was a dynamic personality whose enthusiasm for the work she did, impressed me. I regularly visited the center, learned about her passion for psychiatric social work, saw what the children's needs were and how they could be helped. I observed and participated in simple tasks with the young children. On weekends, when fundraising events took place, I engaged in the planning and layout as well as offering all-round assistance. She obviously took note of my readiness to work with them. At one point, when the American consulate scouted for "kids with promise," to apply for American scholarships to study abroad, Violet was asked if she had any recommendations. She suggested I apply, which I did, but only years later after graduation from university. I wasn't very hopeful. My previous attempt at an application for the American Field Service, despite making the short list and being interviewed by the anthropologist Hilda Kuper, followed by her subsequent very reassuring comments, amounted to a simple final rejection. Only later, when a neighbor, Jack Naidoo, the principal of M. L. Sultan Technical College returned from his visit to the United States, did he tell me that I should not feel despondent because the reason for the rejection was that American Field Service scholarships at the time were only being given to White students. It had nothing to do with the quality of my application.

UNIVERSITY EDUCATION

My girl cousins and friends were being encouraged by their parents to enroll at the Teachers' Training College to take a teaching diploma. They considered this a good career path for girls. My father, on the other hand, steered me away from this option. "You need to get a broader university education. You may find something else that interests you," was his argument. So he took time off from work and arranged an appointment with the student counselor at the University of Natal. The meeting with the counselor took place at Howard College, the White campus of the University of Natal. I could tell that my father, who had never had the opportunity to attend these hallowed buildings, was very excited by the campus, in awe of this potential place of education for me, as well as a little nervous. Little did he know then that this was the "White" campus, not where I would be studying. The counselor, an older White man, was so impressed by the aspirations of a father for his daughter's education that he paid great attention to going over the options, what the courses would be like, in terms that a layperson could understand. By the time we left, we were both sold on the idea. I was the first person in our entire extended family to attend university. No one was prouder of this than my father and mother. Only years later did I learn that he had to borrow funds from his company to pay the fees.

When it came to actual attendance at university, the physical space for the non-European section of the university was in a disused warehouse, located in a small business area of the city, near bus ranks . My expectations of the university up on the hill were to be quickly readjusted. Our classes all took place either very early in the mornings or late in the evenings, since the same lecturers were teaching the White students separately up on the hill during the day. Their teaching loads had to be adjusted to accommodate both schedules. Though we paid the same fees as White students, no sports facilities were available to us. Despite all of this, we had lots of fun. It wasn't long before I met my first boyfriend, who offered to drive me to the Rag Ball, to raise funds for charity. However, dating wasn't part of Indian parents' idea of university, so my arrival at the ball had to be in the company of other girlfriends and innovative means developed to return home.

Having no one else in the family who had been to university, the choice of courses was entirely left to me. I chose English and sociology as my majors, and some courses in Roman-Dutch law, French, Latin, and, of all things, speech and drama. We learned many things in this colonized university setting. Critical literary analysis formed a strong core of the English courses. Never once were we introduced to the idea that we could write original pieces; that we could initiate; that we had agency. Instead, we were introduced to male-dominated English literature over a 3-year period with one session only on F. Scott Fitzgerald's *Great Gatsby* for American literature. Texts from the third world, later referred to as "Commonwealth literature," were nonexistent. I recall in the speech and drama class, playing the role of Antigone, which was a refreshing change. I could relate to the political aspects of the struggle. Yet when it came to my recitation of Wordsworth's poem about daffodils, I was told I didn't show enough excitement at the sight of a hundred golden daffodils. How could I fake it when I'd never seen a daffodil and all I had seen were African daisies!

Undoubtedly there was much to be gained from immersion in great literature of a certain period. A richer education would have established connections with other world literatures and forged links with our experience. Neglected was how we too could "make" knowledge.

Outside of classes, university provided focused opportunities for political discussion and where we each stood on the question of antiapartheid activism. At that time, the White-student–dominated National Union of South African Students (NUSAS) prided itself on a gradualist policy favoring academic integration, bypassing social integration, so we distanced ourselves from them. The Non-European Section of the University of Natal became a point of contact between ANC supporters and Pan-Africanists under the leadership of Robert Sobukwe, a language teacher at Wits University, at the time a White university with very few Non-White students in special faculties. The Pan-Africanists promoted a return of South Africa that they named "Azania" to the indigenous inhabitants. They considered the ANC alliance of White, Colored, and Indian organizations to be an obstacle to the struggle for Black liberation. Heated debates took place between these opposing forces. The Pan-African Congress (PAC)-initiated pass boycott resulted in the police opening fire in Sharpeville in April 1960 on protesters with massive loss of lives and many more injured. For a while, there was a unifying quiet recognition that this marked the failure of peaceful means of protest and the ruthlessness of the enemy with whom we were dealing. We students boycotted lectures for some time.

What did I learn from the courses I took that had lasting value? Many were the lost opportunities. There was an appalling lack of critical awareness of how racial domination, power, and politics worked. At a critical time when we were living in a formal racial polity, where our daily liberties were being curtailed, why were we never introduced to the international literature from societies facing similar issues? Was it because most of this literature was banned? Was it because of who taught us and their lack of political concern? Was it because I had chosen courses such as English, speech, and drama; Latin, French, and Roman-Dutch Law?

One exception to all of this was Leo Kuper, then head of the Sociology Department who did the most to counter the dominant pathos. He refused to teach racially segregated classes and insisted on combining students in the classes he taught. He wrote books on passive resistance analyzing the process used by Gandhi in his campaigns. He invited Pierre van den Berghe to teach in his department, who introduced us to concepts of paternalism and different kinds of domination, the subject of his excellent book *Race and Racism* (1967). He conducted studies of a sugar company's operation to show how race and racism worked within that micro-context. That was the closest we came to a critical education.

At the end of my first degree, I followed my father's advice to take a 1-year postgraduate Teacher Education degree, in case a professional certificate was ever necessary in the future. Prior to that, he arranged a short visit to Mauritius for me to improve my spoken French. Immediately upon graduation, I was offered a position as a high school teacher at my old alma mater, Durban Indian Girls High, teaching English and history. At the same time, I applied for an American scholarship being offered by the Institute of International Education. At the end of my first 6 months of teaching, one day my father showed up at school at the end of the day. He had tears in his eyes as he handed me the letter I had received to say I had won the scholarship to study in America. For a person who had never had such an opportunity, it was a huge success. I was off to begin the new year in the United States in September 1963.

CHAPTER 4

Learning from Gandhi and Mandela

Lessons in Leadership in a Modern World

Education is the most powerful weapon which you can use to change the world.

—Nelson Mandela

The world is my community.

—Mahatma Gandhi

Genuine political literacy eschews romanticizing leaders in favor of grasping social circumstances in which icons evolve in their full complexity. Virtues and vices, strengths and follies characterize even outstanding leaders. As a child of Africa, layered with Indian heritage, I was fortunate to be influenced by Gandhi and Mandela, two moral compasses to the world. In this chapter, I explore the paths they took. Their views evolved over time as did the relationship between their personal experiences and public roles.

What were the contrasting strategies adopted in two similar anticolonial struggles? Gandhi was dealing with external colonialism, while Mandela faced internal colonialism. Where and why did each succeed or fail? Mandela transformed a seemingly escalating racial confrontation into a nominally reconciled, nonracial, unified country, despite the initial endorsement of armed struggle. Gandhi brought about Indian independence from British rule through a sophisticated mobilization of nonviolent resistance, shaming the colonizer. He unfortunately failed to avert a devastating partition along sectarian lines at the cost of a million lives. Race, caste, religion, and gender play a part in the life trajectories of both leaders.

MAHATMA GANDHI (1869-1948)

Gandhi's influence permeated the world vision of my youth at many levels. As far back as I can remember, he was revered in our family because he epitomized peaceful resistance. He gave dignity to those dominated by the illegitimate apartheid rule. As a child, conversations I heard were about this man who came to South Africa clad in a three-piece English suit, eventually becoming an activist and shedding the suit for simple, handmade Indian clothes. He fearlessly stood up to authorities and spoke out against unjust laws. And I recall the dismay of the elders in our family when Gandhi was assassinated by a fellow Hindu.

At high school, my classmate Ela Gandhi, Mahatma Gandhi's granddaughter, invited a few of us to spend a night at her home, located some 15 kilometers from Durban, in the Phoenix settlement that her grandfather had founded on 100 acres of land. Here, Gandhi had switched from being a lawyer to becoming a simple worker living communally, experimenting with conservation, growing his own food, living with minimal possessions, and becoming as self-sufficient as possible. He established a printing press there in 1904, from which the first Indian newspaper, *Indian Opinion,* was published.

I only began to appreciate this background in my later teenage years. What I recall from that visit was the atmosphere of wholesome living that impacted my senses. The tables were of simple, untreated wood. There were bowls of brown sugar at the table. Ela's mother and a few women relatives served us a vegetarian meal, with homemade brown bread and handmade chapatis. The women wore white handwoven cotton saris with simple borders. Their faces showed little emotion, a gentle demure smile almost looking a little sad. Curtains to keep out the scorching sun were also of white handwoven cotton. Later, I learned the history of why everything was handspun and the significance of the spinning loom in pictures of Gandhi. The spinning wheel was the symbol of resistance to British exploitation of locally grown cotton, which was exported to Britain, manufactured into fine cotton, then sent back to be sold with added taxes to the Indian population. One piece of furniture at Gandhi's home stood out as a colonial relic for me: a grand piano. Its presence showed Gandhi's attempt to incorporate different religions and choral traditions in the daily evening prayer sessions. The piano might have been to accompany the daily hymns from different cultural traditions.

Overall, I remember the visit to the home as one of generous hospitality and kindness. At the same time, it brimmed with moral purity. I felt a little unworthy and impure in the face of all this asceticism. Everything seemed so controlled. And yet these values filtered down to us in different ways as I reflected on our lives. The Phoenix settlement project embodied the nucleus of what was to become Gandhi's nonviolent revolutionary movement. At the heart of this project, to build community, lay the foundational work of developing the "inner self" as a prerequisite for political action. People had to be made aware of the consequences of desires that furthered socially and environmentally degrading practices. Gandhi was one of the best examples of "the power of one."

I wondered how my forefathers had received the information in 1893 of a 23-year-old British-educated Indian barrister with a first-class ticket being thrown off a train at Pietermaritzburg Station, denied accommodation, and assaulted. To them, getting pushed off buses and trains was, most likely, not an unusual event. They might have questioned why he even went into a first-class compartment. Did he think he was White? Did he intentionally seek a confrontation to make himself a victim? Was he naive to imagine that his first-class ticket, his English accent and education, or his bourgeois well-tailored suit would protect him and give him a privilege denied to others of his race? He should have known it was "not his place." This is often how oppressed people respond, by knowing their boundaries. They learn how not to transgress these customary limits to avoid conflict. Njabulo Ndebele (1991) expresses this well: "Even under the most oppressive of conditions, people are always trying and struggling to maintain a semblance of normal social order. They will attempt to apply tradition and custom to manage their day-to-day family problems: they will resort to socially acquired behavior patterns to eke out a means of subsistence. They apply systems of values that they know" (p. 49). It was what Gandhi did with this experience of being thrown off the train that made a difference. This was where it all began. He saw this incident in the context of so many other injustices. This was not the moment to be offended enough to return to India, but to take on the cause, to stay and fight along with the powerless.

Instead of depressing us, almost unknowingly, my grandparents and later my parents' generation were strengthened by his dignified response to the indignity he faced. From then on, every incursion on our freedom became an empowering tool. No longer were we individually demeaned, but we were valorized by a motivation to collective resistance. The definition of *us* and *them* immediately redefined *us* on the side of the righteous and *them* as the unquestioning beneficiaries of immoral policies. It is not *we* who should be embarrassed by transgressing immoral laws but the lawmakers who ought to be made aware of the effects of their actions. The traditional distinction between *elite* and *subaltern* took on a different meaning.

I found myself using exactly this logic when taking our daughters, aged 14 and 11, out shopping in Durban in 1984 on one of our annual visits to their grandparents. Apartheid rules were said to be softening. After some shopping, they wanted to sit and have something to eat. Seeing a Wimpy Bar, which had just opened in Durban, we went in. One would have thought we had entered in our underwear. Everyone stared at us. The embarrassed Indian waiter winked at me and whispered, "They don't serve 'us' here!" The African waitresses looked at us angrily communicating nonverbally, "What right have you got to come in here? This is a Whites-only place." There was no sign of compassion or camaraderie for the exclusion of a fellow Non-White. The irony of such situations is that subordinate groups working in places exclusively for Whites, gain a certain amount of deflected status in working there and anyone breaking into this honored realm destroys their "status" as well. I winked back at the Indian waiter and told him it was OK. Our daughters, born and raised in mild-mannered Canada, did not comprehend exactly what was going on. One said, "They're so unfriendly!" I chose to ignore these cues. We seated ourselves at an unoccupied table, upon which the White manageress came up to us and in a very posh English accent said, "I'm sorry we have a liquor license here and don't serve Non-Whites." "Oh," I said, "No worries, we won't be having any alcohol." She replied, "No, we cannot serve you here." Reading my querulous expression, she responded, "I'm sorry, it's not me, I'm English. I'm just following the rules."

By now, my girls were beside themselves with embarrassment. "Just let's go!" they both said. I resisted and wasn't going to leave this place where everyone's eyes were fixed on us. Were we to sheepishly walk out after being rejected? So, I stood up, and said in the clearest speech I could muster, aiming to be heard by the whole restaurant, "All of you who are eating at this restaurant should know that this restaurant will NOT serve people like us. If I were you, I would not eat at such a place." The customers' reddened white faces fell into their soups, not knowing what to do. Not one person supported us. I waited. My parting words were, "And you have shown two young Canadian visitors what kind of a country we are in!" Having heard that the girls were foreigners, the manageress, came back and offered to make us a quick meal. We walked out. Of course, my teenagers were embarrassed for the spectacle I had created. To resist fearlessly came naturally to me. For my girls, good Canadian manners had taught them to be discrete and not create a scene. I said to them, "It's not *we* who have to be embarrassed, it's those people in there. What we have done is to make them think about what they are doing. No one can say they didn't know how apartheid works. And if I had told them you were Canadian, they would have rushed to serve us, but you know I saved that for last as I didn't want exceptions made for what other non-White people cannot enjoy. So forget about being embarrassed. Be proud that we stood up to them."

To this day they have not forgotten this experience and applaud me for it. That very evening we had been invited to the home of an English sugar baron who was on the Buthelezi Commission with my husband. I relayed the story to his very colonial wife and some of the other women. They were shocked by our experience and could not believe this had happened. From their protected enclave, they knew little of the "other South Africa," and politics wasn't what upper-class English ladies dabbled in. In their imperial manner they promised to call the Wimpy Bar to complain of this "bad practice" as if it were a unique occurrence! All the time I was aware that this was not the socially appropriate thing to raise in such rarified company. Yet good manners serve to uphold all kinds of injustices in the world, and we need to learn to break free of them, if we aim at making the invisible visible.

Our indentured minority origins and our local grievances became intertwined with that of India's anticolonial struggles. In fact, the South African experience became the testing ground for the leadership Gandhi was to play in India's anti-colonial project. Paradoxically, Indians in South Africa, while empathetic to the condition of the colonized in India, identified primarily with the country of their adoption. There was never a case of divided loyalty. They had made their choice to leave India, and South Africa had become home, despite all the outrageous laws against them. Even after the completion of their 5-year indenture, most chose to remain and take the offer of land in lieu of passage back to India. New restrictions were imposed. Free Indians, now seen as a threat to White traders, were refused trading licenses and required to pay a 3-pound tax, which most could ill afford. Numerous other pieces of legislation such as the "Ghetto Act" restricted Indian ownership of land in certain areas, declared marriages conducted under traditional rites to be null and void, and rendered the progeny illegitimate and therefore unable to exercise the rights of citizenship in the country.

Through shared political exclusion and discrimination, Gandhi was also able to unify an Indian community composed of wealthier as well as poorer segments, and divided along religious and linguistic lines: Muslims, Hindus, Christians, and Zoroastrians who spoke a range of home languages including Hindi, Tamil, Urdu, Telugu, and Gujarati. The diverse community mobilized as one in a series of passive resistance campaigns.

Contradicting those who described "passive resistance" as the strategy of the weak, Gandhi pointed out his strategy of "Satyagraha" as the power of truth. Exposure to Tolstoy's ideas in 1909, when he was working as a lawyer in South Africa, led him to consolidate the view that individual conscience is superior to any form of government and a force to be developed. Unlike Tolstoy who despised politics, Gandhi saw the potential of personal morality as a political instrument, which he mobilized. He even named his second community development, in Johannesburg, Tolstoy Farm.

As a child, I recall the mobilization of women as equal partners in campaigns. Gandhi's wife, Kasturbai, had played a much-overlooked but significant role alongside him. My mother joined a women's group in preparation for one of the civil disobedience campaigns. They were told to anticipate as part of prison routines the requirement for women to strip naked each morning to be examined by the wardens. This, I recall from conversations between the women, ranked highest in their fears. Unfortunately, in the end, my mother had to pull out of the campaign, since my younger sister, then only a year old, fell ill and the person who was to care for us while she was imprisoned was no longer able to provide the support my father would have needed while he was at work. One of her closest friends with whom she had "trained" in preparation for the arrest, Panjarathnam Pillay, lived upstairs in our apartment building. She was imprisoned for civil disobedience for a month in 1947 on that campaign. My mother envied her strength and courage.

Gandhi influenced our community also in seemingly simple ways by altering the habits of everyday life. He demonstrated, through the symbolic use of the spinning wheel, the value of creating and making clothing from handspun cotton. He shamed us for consuming without giving thought to the genesis of imported goods in our subjugation and to the sustainability of the environment. The wearing of handspun cotton and refusal to consume manufactured goods was not totally embraced by Indians in South Africa, who seemed to follow a midway path. Many considered such a focus as impeding progress in an industrializing world. And yet, already then, Gandhi warned against the consequences of energy-intensive and resource-exploitative practices of Western industrialization. His publication of the newspaper *Indian Opinion* in four languages and extensive writing and recording extolled the importance of discipline in reading and writing as regular activity. He published some 90 volumes in his lifetime on the theory underlying his strategy of defiance and its development. He read widely and was influenced by a broad range of international sources from Tolstoy to Ruskin. As opposed to an inward-turning chauvinism, his approach was always to learn from others. He drew on his traditional roots, yet recognized and welded together key ideas gained from Western political theories. This meant a constant openness to seeking out the best from all knowledge the world had to offer. In this regard his anticolonial struggle differed from some university protests today of removing all reminders of colonialism, even burning books and art from these sources. While valuing cultural and religious diversity, Gandhi was uncompromising in his view that the state should be secular. He inveighed against institutionalizing any one of the religious or cultural groups as state-sponsored, which the Indian Prime Minister Modi ignores today. For Gandhi, religion was strictly part of the private realm, as is the case in most Western democracies. At the same time, he was not against the teaching of religion in schools. Indeed, he promoted religious education, provided it was done in an open, tolerant, respectful manner promoting interreligious dialogue. Religious pluralism was inherent in his references to literature from the Bible and the Koran, as well as to his roots in Hindu classics of the *Bhagavad Gita,* and later to the Tamil Thirukural, which, ironically, a non-Indian, Tolstoy, had introduced to him. He also had a limited tolerance for unthinking adherence to rituals, without some careful consideration of the meaning of such ceremonies. By introducing a special kind of reflective secularism he encouraged people to examine being bounded by rituals as opposed to being open to interrogating the underlying meaning of why and what they were doing. A lasting legacy was his development of a national identification. Anticolonial resistance had a unifying effect on people hailing from different regions of India, who might otherwise have been caught up in divisive ethnolinguistically based local identifications and even secessionism. His inclusive idea of God was that of a higher being, which appealed to a diverse population. His guiding motto, God is Truth, as the foundation of Satyagraha, extolled the power of truth. In South Africa, he brought together people from different linguistic and economic backgrounds to work together toward a common goal. One wonders why neither Africans nor White people were included in these joint campaigns. Was it racist? Was it simply strategic, to begin working with the familiar, namely the population he knew best, which had specific laws directed against them around which they could mobilize?

Perhaps most critical of all was his way of looking at the oppressor, not as an enemy, but as someone who needed to be taught empathy by understanding the effects of their domination and to be moved by the resistance of those affected. He impressed on the consciousness of the subordinates, that we are never "poor" or "downtrodden." We have either the choice to resist or to collaborate in our subjugation. All these strains were to become infused as part of our education. It lifted us from being second-class citizens and victims.

Gandhi's vision for independent India also extended beyond the territorial realm. He rejected the notion of a "clash of civilizations" and sought to build bridges with the British. He saw no reason why cross-cultural goodwill—an idea close to Mandela's heart—couldn't be revitalized and sustained. Without his global perspective, India arguably would not have been an active participant and partner in the Commonwealth. Gandhi explored many faiths and learned a great deal from the ideals of Islam and from Christianity, especially the notion of human rights. Yet he did not convert but sought to draw upon each and weld them together to reach many people across faiths. He always held the view of "let the influences of many faiths waft through the windows of my home, but let me not be swept away by any of them."

In our family, we were never taught to dislike White people as perpetrators and beneficiaries of apartheid. We encountered White people in many different locations, as fellow resisters, as poor Whites, as family friends, as arrogant oppressors. This made it difficult to generalize. It was the system of racial discrimination that we opposed.

Gandhi had many opponents and detractors. As David Hardiman (2004) summarizes it, "He was accused of being an irresponsible trouble maker by his colonial masters, a destroyer of social harmony by Indian traditionalists, a backward-looking crank by modernizers and progressives, an authoritarian leader by those within the movement who resented his style of leadership, a Hindu chauvinist by many Muslims, and a defender of high-caste elitism by lower-caste activists" (p. 4).

His ideas about sexual control as a prerequisite for inner control before committing to political activism have been heavily criticized. While his contemporary Freud was diagnosing sexual repression as causes of neurosis and promoting more sexual freedom, Gandhi was reining in sexual freedom as harnessing control over the body. He was criticized for his authoritarian leadership within the movement, particularly toward women. Gandhi has been accused of being condescending toward women, of even expressing the view that they were best suited to the private sphere of the home. While this was indeed his view at some points, it was also a prevailing sentiment of the time. But Gandhi acknowledged that his views were evolving all the time. If this view had persisted, he would not have been successful in incorporating, on equal terms, women's mobilization initiatives in the 1913 Satyagraha movement against legislation declaring Indian traditional marriages illegal and levying heavy taxation on the formerly indentured (Hiralal, 2010, p. 4). He was instrumental in identifying and having Sarojini Naidu, feisty poet and writer, installed as the first woman president of India.

Noteworthy was the systematic educational approach to the struggles he faced. Gradual and incremental beginnings with petitions, deputations, and endless communications to express grievances preceded concerted action of a more forceful collective nature. His communications were always dialogic, seeking out the possibility of dialogue to arrive at a common resolution to problems to be solved. The theme of "Experiments with Truth" indicates that this approach was a work in progress, always admitting when and how he had failed (Gandhi, 1927).

The use of wit and symbolic violation of the colonizer's dress code are often ways in which Gandhi challenged powerholders. When asked what he thought of Western civilization, his oft-quoted response was, "I think it would be a good idea!" Another case where he challenged norms in formal settings was when he had to attend negotiating meetings with British heads of government. He arrived dressed not in formal wear as was the dress code, but in a *dhoti* (loincloth) made of handspun cotton wearing homemade sandals. On yet another occasion the meeting was set up on a day when Gandhi was on a fast, having taken a vow of silence. On this occasion, he handwrote all his responses throughout the entire meeting.

His use of symbolism in politics is said to have alienated Muslims by his use of Hindu symbols. Eventually he was accused of making partition between India and Pakistan unavoidable. When he contested traditional labeling of lower castes as "Pariahs," referring to them as *Harijans* or "children of God" and embraced them as members of his small community, he was criticized for being condescending and paternalistic. Lower-caste activists accused him of being a defender of high-caste elitism.

In South Africa he was criticized for not including Africans in his campaigns and for using derogatory terminology to refer to Africans. Guha (2013) points out that Gandhi behaved in ways that quite rightly were considered racist and sexist, common views at the time. That he had no social or professional contact with Africans during the 2 decades of his time in South Africa was a crucial blemish on his otherwise remarkable life trajectory. Often overlooked in this view is in 1904, when Gandhi established an ashram in Phoenix in Durban, where he set up a press for his newspaper *Indian Opinion,* he developed close relationships with the head of the industrial school, John Langalibalele Dube, the first president of the African National Congress. Dube's first weekly called *Ilanga lase Natal* was printed on the press of *Indian Opinion* and the people from his school often visited the ashram.

Despite these critiques, Gandhi's development of the ideas of "moral power" and "shaming" as tools for resistance continue to resonate in the world. For Indians in South Africa, his most powerful passive resistance campaigns succeeded in mobilizing both men and women indentured laborers.

In India, he campaigned successfully to mobilize people of all classes and castes to go on the Salt March in 1930. It entailed a long march from his ashram near Ahmedabad to the sea at Dandi to extract the salt. Each grabbed a handful as their own, free of the taxation that was being imposed on their purchases of salt. The power of this simple defiance of a colonial imposition impacted deeply on the country. It mobilized people to bring about justice in accessing what was their rightful resource, through peaceful civil disobedience.

When one considers how differently minorities such as the Japanese diaspora in the United States responded to their internment by Roosevelt's executive order to vacate their confiscated homes and move to internment camps, one is tempted to reflect on comparisons of victim behavior in two different political situations. In February 1942, about 120,000 people of Japanese ancestry, two-thirds of whom were U.S. citizens, were stripped of their possessions and removed from their homes. Some resisted by refusing to enlist, by answering "No" to the two questions they were expected to answer affirmatively: (1) Were they willing to serve in the U.S. armed forces on combat duty whenever ordered to do so?; and (2) Would they agree to swear unqualified allegiance and pledge to faithfully defend the United States from attacks by foreign or domestic forces? For the most part, they were in such disbelief about the unimaginable reality they experienced, that they failed to protest and resigned themselves to *shikata ga nai,* meaning "it can't be helped." Many felt the way vulnerable minorities often self-implicate, that it had something to do with themselves. They were simply not American enough. (See the novel on this experience by Okada, 1978.)

This situation contrasts sharply with that of Indians in South Africa who, with the aid of Gandhian redefinition of their political exclusion, strengthened their resolve to resist unjust laws, and not to blame themselves for having failed. In a way, the South African struggle served as a microcosm of the issues that Gandhi faced in India with its linguistic, regional, and religious divides. South Africa prepared an insignificant, unsuccessful Indian lawyer to become a leader of one of the greatest anti-colonial initiatives in the world. Gandhi's absolute honesty about being no genius is evident when he describes himself. In a 1937 speech he looks back on his early life:

> At school the teachers did not consider me a very bright boy. They knew that I was a good boy, but not a bright boy. I never knew first class and second class. I barely passed. I was a dull boy. I could not even speak properly. Even when I went to South Africa, I went only as a clerk. (Gandhi, 1999)

In this, he holds out the possibility for ordinary people to make significant contributions in the world.

What Gandhi left us through his lived example, was a deep set of guiding values to work together across cultural, religious, and caste lines. More importantly, he laid the foundation of precepts by which to redefine ourselves in navigating the oppressive situation in which we lived as a disenfranchised, constantly harassed, Indian minority.

NELSON MANDELA (1918–2013)

Like Gandhi, Nelson Mandela also faced hurdles in education. In a slightly different vein, Mandela struggled with his law studies. In 1943 when he enrolled at Wits University, Professor Hahlo advised him against taking that course of studies as he was unlikely to succeed. As many self-fulfilling prophecies go, Mandela did, in fact, fail miserably in his first attempt to study law, though he subsequently made up for it by a change of institutions later in his life.

As teenagers we grew up with the memory of our true leaders being imprisoned for what they believed. Our longtime family associate, Fatima Meer, a close friend of the Mandelas, went to visit Nelson Mandela in prison on Robben Island whenever the Mandela family freed up one of their entitled visits and she was granted permission to stand in. We were in awe of her access. All the time he was imprisoned, he was our hope as someone who stood up to authority with conviction. Mandela was the icon of the South African resistance against oppression and the transformation from a racist apartheid society to an open and inclusive non-racial nation. At the age of 46, in June 1964 he was sentenced to life imprisonment, which lasted 27 years. Before the judge handed down his verdict, with everyone expecting a death sentence, Mandela did not plead for mercy, but made his most famous confession:

> During my lifetime I have dedicated myself to this struggle of the African people. I have fought against white domination and I have fought against black domination. I have cherished the ideal of a democratic and free society in which all persons live together in harmony and with equal opportunities. It is an ideal which I hope to live for and to achieve. But if needs be, it is an ideal for which I am prepared to die. (http://www.historyplace.com/speeches/mandela.htm)

Mandela's unique style led him to become a modern world leader of a different genre from that of Gandhi, yet similar in depth and groundedness. Mandela was baptized as a Methodist, but well ensconced in the traditional world of his father's people. Raised in an environment where chiefs were vested with traditional authority, he must have observed in daily dealings the role of participatory consensus building, listening, respecting, accounting, and sympathizing, crucial attitudes involved in the effective management of leadership.

One of his earliest politicizing moments arose during his circumcision rite at the age of 16. In these weeklong ceremonies, young Xhosa boys are initiated to manhood. At the celebratory event afterward, Chief Meligqili in addressing the circumcised youth, invoked their newly acquired adult status by reminding them that they were still a subjugated people:

> For we Xhosas, and all black South Africans,
> are a conquered people. We are slaves in our own
> country. We are tenants on our own soil. We have
> no strength, no power, no control over our own
> destiny in the land of our birth. They [the initiates]
> will go to the cities where they will live
> in shacks and drink cheap alcohol all because
> we have no land. . . . They will cough their lungs
> out deep in the bowels of the white man's mines,
> destroying their health, . . . so that the white man
> can live a life of unequalled prosperity. . . . the
> children of Ngubengcuka, the flower of the Xhosa
> nation, are dying. (Mandela, 1994, p. 31)

With these formative exhortations in mind, Mandela's approach to passive resistance differed from Gandhi's, but not without respect for what Gandhi had introduced. In his autobiography, Mandela (1994) comments on his feelings about the futility of passive resistance in the face of increasing repressiveness of government. The time for passive resistance had ended. "Nonviolence was a useless strategy and could never overturn a White minority regime bent on retaining its power at any cost. At the end of the day, violence was the only weapon that would destroy apartheid and we must be prepared, in the near future, to use that weapon" (p. 137). For Mandela, his choice of violence as opposed to nonviolence was a strategy not a principle. Strategy depends on changing circumstances; principle amounts to a lasting ethical commitment.

Comparing the South African situation with India's, Mandela (1994) saw Gandhi dealing with a foreign power that ultimately was more realistic, farsighted, and susceptible to moral reasoning, at least in its liberal sections. That was not the case with the more monolithic Afrikaner nationalists at the time. "Nonviolent passive resistance is effective as long as your opposition adheres to the same rules as you do. But if peaceful protest is met with violence, its efficacy is at an end. For me nonviolence was not a moral principle but a strategy; there is no moral goodness in using an ineffective weapon" (p. 137).

However, he was to be proven wrong when a "negotiated revolution" between two one-time adversaries took place without a civil war. Mandela greatly facilitated the process through his realistic assessment of the changed political forces at play in the 1980s. While the insurrectionists in the ANC insisted that what was not won on the battlefield could not be won at the negotiating table, Mandela persuaded the movement that neither side could win on the battlefield without destroying the country in a protracted civil war. In this stalemate, negotiations with opponents promised the only solution. The lesson to be learned from this insight is that demonizing a hated enemy as evil is counterproductive to peaceful coexistence. Evil demands to be eliminated. However, if one has to live with a collective enemy in the same country, elimination and retribution offer no hope for reconciliation, unless the enemy is to be redefined as a political adversary.

Politics as a compromise was also assisted by the secular definition of the South African conflict. Both sides viewed apartheid as racial privilege maintenance. Yet power and privilege are negotiable while religious absolutes are not. Religious doctrines cannot be shared by a mutual give and take process. In Syria, for example, the ruling Shiite minority of Alawites perceives their Sunni Muslim majority as "heretics," not citizens with equal rights. Political ascendancy of such a majority is perceived by the minority as an existential threat. When an American government therefore requires "regime change" of the Assad regime as a precondition for peace, it falls on deaf ears. The threatened minority fights for survival by all means possible, even with poison gas, regardless of human rights violations.

In Iraq, a similar situation existed in reverse: a Shiite majority, discriminating against a Sunni minority. In Modi's India, an indoctrinated Hindu majority discriminates against Muslims, despite the inclusive Hinduism of Gandhi. When Mandela referred abroad to "our people," he meant all South Africans.

In Mandela's world view, only a freely negotiated political compromise guarantees peace. I learned from the negotiated settlement that history is never predetermined and nothing is inevitable, as orthodox Marxists assumed. The unexpected can supersede taken-for-granted outcomes, and human agency must not be underestimated. Mandela's years in prison seemed not to be in vain. There were always unintended consequences. His incarceration enabled the opportunity to read, reflect, and strategize with other prisoners dedicated to a common cause and subject to similar circumstances; the development of a more nuanced understanding of power at all levels, from the power of the governing regime to the power of the lowly prison wardens; recognition that they were in it for the long haul and therefore had to strive for better terms for their day-to-day survival. This he did without compromising or kowtowing to privilege. He learned to "read" and understand more deeply the prison wardens, their lives and needs, and to turn this knowledge to the prisoners' advantage. This entailed seeing them as human beings too, deprived of normal lives, isolated on an island, as less educated even than those they guarded, as lacking everyday skills when it came to dealing with the law and struggling with the English language, which limited their communication with others. Yet they also had the power to make everyday life for the prisoners more tolerable. Given the communication gap, Mandela learned Afrikaans, the stigmatized language, associated with the state's imperious attempts to impose it on subordinate groups. When asked why, he mentioned that it was a disadvantage not to know a language spoken by most Whites and Coloreds. Mandela added an emotional component: "When you speak Afrikaans, you know, you go straight to their hearts" (Stengel, 2012, p. 135).

Beyond these instrumental reasons was the Gandhian appeal to delve into the psyche of opponents and seek out the humanity within. Mandela (1994) felt strongly that "the oppressor must be liberated just as surely as the oppressed. A man who takes away another man's freedom is a prisoner of hatred, he is locked behind the bars of prejudice and narrow-mindedness. I am not truly free if I am taking away someone else's freedom, just as when my freedom is taken from me. The oppressed and the oppressor alike are robbed of their humanity" (p. 544).

That Mandela was endowed with charisma was unquestioned, notwithstanding his sometimes wooden style of speech delivery. "Mandela magic" represented a friendly face of hope to a decolonizing struggling continent, where one leader after another failed to sustain hope. Mandela filled this gap. Here was a man who put a positive spin on life, despite 27 years of incarceration. The expected bitterness and quest for revenge was totally absent. Some Blacks interpreted this magnanimity as the "Stockholm syndrome," the identification of a hostage with the overwhelming power of the hostage-taker. Many White South Africans absolved themselves of their racism by praising Mandela. His smile and gestures of reconciliation radiated hope.

Charisma-driven leadership always poses the threat of personality cult and demagoguery. Before Mandela's time, Max Weber had raised the question of whether charisma could be converted to a more routinized or bureaucratized form, to avoid the cult of personality. Mandela carefully avoided a personality cult by subjecting himself to joint decision making as part of a collective leadership in the African National Congress. As Jeremy Waldron (2019) writes on the constitutionalization of charisma:

> Someone like Mandela didn't just take and exercise power under the auspices of his own personality. He got together with others to put in place an enduring system of authority, a system that would house the aspirations of his successors, even his opponents, in future years. And he did this not by means of secret machinations, but by proclaiming a public set of rules and values, with a view to their being accepted by the people as a whole. (p. 12)

When the ANC Executive Committee decided to require the national rugby team to change and remove their tricots, which were reminders of the apartheid era, Mandela insisted on reversal. Recognizing the importance of symbolism in a sports-crazy society, Mandela donned the Springboks tricot and cap when he presented the World Cup to South African rugby captain Francois Pienaar after a dramatic game against New Zealand, which the South African team won 15–12 in extra time. Since this magic moment in the Johannesburg Ellis Park stadium on June 24, 1995, many skeptical White fans felt reconciled and no longer unfolded the old Republican flag in place of the new flag. These gestures demonstrated his retention of autonomous judgment in order to win over skeptical groups. He even invited himself to a much-publicized tea with the widow of the architect of apartheid, Hendrik Verwoerd.

Keeping an open mind on politically contested issues and being prepared to change one's position on the basis of new information avoids ideological dogmatism, which results in a blindness to opportunities for change. Mandela (2011) displayed the rare capacity for introspection to the extent of self-deprecation. He admitted being "appalled by the pedantry, artificiality and lack of originality" (p. 45) of his early writings. Humility shines through the confession that he once "was backward politically" (p. 43), but by implication, that determined self-teaching could reverse ignorance. Although he had more than enough reason for self-pity, Mandela never wallowed in victimhood but stressed agency. The prisoner rejected his own liberation offered when acceptance of release (to the Transkei or by renouncing violence) could compromise political principles. An acute sense of reality inveighs against grandstanding and posturing. Instead of empowering a revolutionary organization, it could lead to delusions about the adversary and wishful thinking. An illegitimate regime is not necessarily an unstable one. This insight requires being flexible and dispassionate enough to peruse the logic of one's adversary and to utilize the cleavages and contradictions within that group. Cultivating the ability to seek out the shared interests between adversaries and establishing common ground so that both sides experience change as advantageous underlay the ingenious negotiating of the peaceful transformation. Mandela foremost defined leadership as the art of compromise. Like Gandhi, Mandela's use of wit to deal with complex questions was admirable. George Bizos, his family lawyer, told the story of Judge Bekker asking Mandela sarcastically, "You want one man, one vote? Would you settle for anything less?" Nelson would evade the question saying, "Well you know, I can't speak for the organization. But make us an offer, you know, and we'll consider it" (Maharaj & Kathrada, 2006, p. 82).

Equality of opportunity, with the hope of ensuing emancipatory effects for all, was a prevalent theme throughout Mandela's philosophy. Yet, decades after his release from prison, similar patterns of educational outcomes reminiscent of the past persist along racial lines. There are personal lessons that can be drawn from Mandela's approach to learning and life in general. He cultivated intuitively what psychologists refer to as a "growth mindset" (Dweck, 2016), thriving on challenges, avoiding victimization, and turning challenges and failures into opportunities. In our schools we too rarely teach with a growth mindset or help students turn around failure and see opportunities for change. Schools that are segregated racially or economically with regard to resources or educational practices that track or stream curriculum on the basis of perceived ability differences serve to stereotype students in ways that fail to engage them as equal citizens. The teaching of agency is often reserved for some students, not others, and the focus on competition rather than cooperation does not equip youth for compromise and a commitment to the common good. Rhona Weinstein (2002), in her book *Reaching Higher: The Power of Expectations in Schooling,* refers to two different achievement cultures, one that selects talent (looking for the most qualified, usually those with high-status attributes) versus the one that develops the talent of all. The latter was the goal toward which Mandela was dedicated and the philosophy and organization of our schools ought to mirror this.

Mandela utilized critical self-reflection to take place on many levels to transform praxis. He valued critical feedback and encouraged knowledge of contrary perceptions to be probed. One such example occurred toward the end of his presidency, as Martin Hall (2009) recalls an encounter in 1999. Mandela invited the vice chancellor and 20 faculty members from the University of Cape Town to a frank discussion of the successes and failures during his time in office. During a 3-hour session the issues raised and commented upon included economic policy, reconciliation, and the epidemic development of HIV and AIDS in the country, which he had not addressed until quite late. Through this session, Mandela not only demonstrated his respect for research and informed criticism, but also the value of teamwork and consensual decision making by recognizing adversarial opinions.

The transitional experience from apartheid to a nonracial new South Africa through the Truth and Reconciliation Commission (TRC) posed critical questions. Grounded in the rationale that since we continue to live in the same space, it was critical to avoid a bloody revolution, which might occur through the pursuit of retribution for past injustice. The TRC sought a national project of peaceful reconciliation. Through public hearings and airing of victims' stories, amnesty would be granted to perpetrators for divulging past crimes. Knowledge of the past would become public. Healing would follow revealing. Many questions arose: What does this mean for forgiveness and reconciliation? Is it a sign of weakness to show compassion to the perpetrators? Does it mean a numbing of the senses and a compromise without a free and open inquiry? In victims' narration of their own stories under great pain with little compensation were they being used yet again to simply meet the grand design of peaceful reconciliation? While only gross human rights violations were being addressed, what of the beneficiaries of systemic discrimination? Were we yet again seeking to demonstrate how humane Black people can be to understand the deeply seated "goodness" in even the most horrid of perpetrators and murderers? However, Njabulo Ndebele (2007) speaks of the TRC as "having moved us from repression to expression; that there is something inherently reflective about memory . . . (which) stands to guarantee us occasions for some serious moments of reflection. The TRC lifted the veil of secrecy and state induced blindness" (p. 85),

Mandela's most important pedagogical legacies demonstrate the moral high ground he held, despite conformity pressure. His steadfast support of the Truth and Reconciliation Commission flew in the face of his successor's criticism that the TRC had criminalized the liberation struggle by equating ANC violations in a just struggle with the atrocities of an unjust apartheid regime. Mandela firmly supported the widely accepted distinction between a *just war* and *justice in war*. Like Desmond Tutu and the TRC argued, even in a just war, certain avoidable actions, like killing of civilians or prisoners, constitute injustice. Mandela spoke out against the abuses of the Mugabe regime when the ANC government avoided public criticism or even supported Zimbabwe, because Mugabe was popular among Black South Africans and government figures benefitted from the alliance. One wishes that other ANC executives had followed Mandela's lead and he himself had broken more often with his self-imposed "organizational discipline."

Toward the end of his life and after his death, Mandela was denigrated by being called a "sellout" by a militant minority because of his pragmatic approach to an unwinnable victory in a stalemate, preventing the destruction of the country in a civil war like Syria. Mandela was downgraded as being seduced by "monopoly capitalism" in an unfinished revolution. If students learn the lessons about compromise in democracies, nonviolence, and principled moral leadership, historical heroes like Mandela, Gandhi, or Martin Luther King have nevertheless triumphed.

The legacy of this complex figure will live on, idealized by most and reviled by few, hopefully to be dissected in all his virtues and flaws by politically literate analysts. After all, it was Mandela who massively contributed to a new South Africa emerging peacefully during a crucial historical moment, by persuading his own skeptical movement while pacifying and marginalizing a White right-wing threat to the change of political power. That the "imagined liberation" (Adam & Moodley, 2015) has faded and floundered in the current South Africa is not Mandela's shortcoming. His vision and legacy remind us to revive it.

When I was an international student in the United States (1963–1965), there were frequent occasions when international students were called upon to contribute knowledge about our countries of origin to U.S. audiences. Participants proudly showed national flags and some sang their national anthems, explained their meaning and elaborated on the significance of the symbols. At this time, I became acutely aware of having been raised as a Non-White South African with no pride in either the national anthem or flag of my country. After all, I was a member of a disenfranchised minority—who couldn't cast my first vote until the age of 53. The South African flag under apartheid embodied White supremacy since 1652. It represented the legitimacy of their right to self-determination. We "Non-White" people were nowhere represented in that flag. I identified with the liberation movement (ANC), as I did with its rallying anthem "Nkosi Sikelele Afrika"(God Bless Africa), but both were illegal and largely unknown in the United States at the time. When I reflect upon this state of nonidentification, it was a double-edged sword. On the one hand, it is sad to grow up not identifying with one's country and being proud of one's place in it as a citizen. But all too often along with this comes aggressive nationalism, which has been the source of much conflict in the world. Being free of such unquestioning identification also had its advantages. But being a critical outsider, when one can no longer influence happenings in the land of one's birth, always poses the likelihood of political alienation, powerlessness, victimhood, and cynicism. I didn't have a happy story to tell when my turn came up, because at that time it was not so clear that South Africa could become what it did in 1990 with the release of Mandela. Little did I think I would one day dare to send a copy of the book I would coauthor in 1986 with my husband, Heribert Adam, *South Africa Without Apartheid: Dismantling Racial Domination,* to Mandela, then imprisoned at Pollsmoor on the outskirts of Cape Town. Apart from rare family visits, nobody was allowed to see Mandela, and only decades old pictures of him circulated in the liberal media.

The story of our "encounter" with Mandela through our book started with H. W. van der Merwe, the respected Afrikaans-speaking head of the Institute of Intercultural Studies at the University of Cape Town. In 1986 he went on a sabbatical when Heribert was appointed acting head, and we spent a year at the little institute cottage on campus. H.W., an unassuming Quaker academic of absolute integrity, was one of the first non-ANC Afrikaners who had initiated contact with the Lusaka ANC. Winnie Mandela, on her way to Robben Island often stayed at the home of H.W., and Mandela occasionally communicated about family matters through H.W. At our request, H.W. arranged a meeting with Brigadier Munroe, the head of Pollsmoor, strategically excluding myself as a Black woman in a racially mixed marriage. Both "professors" in formal suits and ties were cordially received for tea with the Brigadier. The strategy was to hand over two unsigned copies of the book, one for the Commandant and the other for "his famous prisoner." With the promise "to seek permission from Pretoria," we had given up hope after 2 months waiting in vain. Yet another month later, a hand-written letter arrived. It was written on a lined notebook page. The handwriting was very neat, almost schoolboyish, every *i* dotted and *t* crossed. It was from Nelson Mandela, thanking us for the gift of the book, which made him take a "more than usual interest" in us, and requesting if we would come by the prison to sign the copy to him, personally. Needless to say, we were thrilled. We thought this might be an invitation to meet with him. However, when we arrived there after arranging another appointment with the Brigadier, Munroe said he was not allowed under prison regulations to let us meet Mr. Mandela in person. The book was brought to us from the prison library by a warden. We signed it with a warm dedication, and it was then handed back. It was a chilling experience being so close and yet so distant from the resistance leader. Four years later, in the dusk on February 11, 1990, we saw him for the first time after his final release on the balcony of City Hall, having waited in a large excited crowd the whole afternoon. Much later, upon our second meeting, his witty introduction with his usual joke was, "*You* may not remember, but we've met before!"

CHAPTER 5

A Visiting Student in the United States

I entered the United States as an international student—or foreign student, as we were called then—with a scholarship from the Institute of International Education in 1963 to pursue a master's degree in sociology. My first point of entry was New York, from where I traveled to Connecticut for an orientation program at Yale University. During this time, we were also offered a seminar in economics and development. The month I spent there was one of my most memorable experiences. It was my first exposure to a society where I could sit where I wanted to, eat in any restaurant, and visit any theater. There was no color bar, unlike the country I had just left. At the same time, I quickly observed the racialized nature of the dividing line between two parts of New Haven where Yale University was located. The international students in our cohort were from many countries, and every day I felt so very fortunate to be in this situation. We visited host families eager to show us what the United States was all about. Reluctant children were brought to meet us in front of a large globe displaying different continents. One child looked at me and said, "She is one of the good Indians! Isn't she?" The undergraduate student dormitories in which we stayed were normally for the exclusive use of male students only; we were the first cohort of women to appropriate the place. At the end of our stay we had 2 days to spend overnight in New York before heading off to our destinations across the country. I must have looked helpless waiting at the bus station, when the relatives of a Panamanian student who had come to fetch her, drove back and asked me if I would like to stay with them. I had met the student on several occasions during our stay and was quite pleased to do that. They drove a huge Cadillac and lived in a fairly smart section of Harlem in a very spacious apartment. I learned that her brother-in-law was a private investigator, which explained why he had so many cameras in the house. They were very kind and generous. After 2 nights I traveled to Michigan. Paulus Mohome, a fellow student from Lesotho, was there to meet me, for which I was very grateful. I was to spend the next year at Michigan State University with lodgings at Owen Hall, a beautiful graduate residence with many international students.

The Department of Sociology office space was at Berkey Hall, where I shared a cubicle with eight other graduate students. I was the only woman. No one complained in those days about feeling unsafe. I certainly didn't feel threatened. When

57

the frustration level with our work was high we went out to play some table tennis in the hallway. I loved the shocked look on the faces of Americans on days when I wore a sari and would play just as comfortably. They freaked out when I would land a sound smash across the table with no inhibitions . . . not what a nice Indian woman was supposed to do! I surprised people too when the winter came, because I just as easily switched to Western clothes, which was seen as assimilating too quickly, especially for the anthropologists who studied India and "knew all about Indians." They knew little about my kind of hybrid Indian born on African soil and educated in colonial South Africa. Their paradigms didn't allow them to shift from the essentialist frames they had acquired in their study of "those people."

After my 1st year was over, my scholarship was extended for a 2nd year. I shared a house with an American graduate student, who had worked with the peace corps in Dacca, then East Pakistan, and now Bangladesh. She never went out much. Years later after I had left, she came out openly as lesbian, though I had no idea of this when we were housemates. She also must have been wondering about this deviant Indian woman, when I went out to the local pub with my fellow graduate students after we had finished working at around 9 p.m. and came home late.

As a group, we had fun over a beer, which wasn't my favorite, but which I nevertheless sipped. One of the students was Saghir Ahmad, a Pakistani who was very helpful in my initial adaptation to the department. He invited me for Pakistani meals to his apartment, which he shared with three other Pakistani students. He was always full of good political questions and knowledgeable about developments in the third world, and on Pakistan, in particular. Of course, apartheid never ceased to engage people in how such control could continue through the domination of a majority by a minority. Other interesting students were Paulo Ammassari, an Italian industrial sociologist; John Stoekel, a midwestern American; and Eugenio Fonseca from Costa Rica, who seemed to have grandiose illusions about being sought after as a potential leader in exile. Richard Sturgis, a Mormon who occupied the desk beside mine, had a healthy diet of carrot and celery sticks or apple pieces that provided a backdrop of a daily crunching choir.

Later additions were Alan Steeves, who came from rural Ontario and invited me to go ice skating after a meal at his dorm. I will never forget the gusto with which he placed six glasses of milk on his own tray before collecting his meal, and insisted on putting three more on mine, my protests about it being too much notwithstanding. "I grew up with the cows," he said as he emptied my tray of the precious liquid. At the skating rink, I must have made a hilarious picture since I had no idea of how to tread on ice. To his credit, after I fell several times, he graciously guided me around the rink, when my skinny Indian ankles could hold up long enough. This was certainly a memorable outing.

The latest addition to the department was a Glaswegian from Scotland. Maxwell Flood, an industrial sociologist who had previously been at Oxford University, I believe at a college that aimed at offering working-class students an opportunity to enter their hallowed terrain. The gossip mill spread that he experienced severe culture shock when he enrolled in the doctoral program at Michigan State University. He thought he was coming to an English-speaking country, but no one understood him when he spoke with his Glasgow accent. What was required of graduate students was 2 years of course work and a qualifying exam before he could get to work on his dissertation. Of course, Maxwell found this "utter rubbish." Oxford would never require these stumbling blocks, which he considered "a waste of time." The American faculty in the department were intimidated by what they thought was his English background, especially his Oxford experience, as well as his knowledge of the literature on labor law, so they quickly yielded to his demands to be exempt from some of the course requirements. As two colonials, he and I shared similar humor, and I found bantering with him to be great fun—until one day this somehow got a little out of hand. I had to attend a conference in Chicago and drove down with a history professor who organized a session on Africa on which I was a panelist. Maxwell had somehow tracked me down. I was awakened in the early hours of the morning to a phone call, telling me that he had traveled by train and was in Chicago. He wanted to see me. I could tell from his speech that he had been drinking, and I was terrified. I said I had no intention of seeing him, and would meet him when I was back in East Lansing. Fearing that he might show up in the hotel lobby at breakfast, I mentioned to the organizer of the session, as a precaution, that I might encounter an unpleasant situation and asked if he would be available to help me out if necessary. True enough, Maxwell, by now sobered up but still reeking of alcohol, came up to my table at breakfast and said, "The only reason you will have nothing to do with me is because of my class background—because I come from the *worrrking* class of Glasgow." I asked him politely to leave. I was accustomed to encountering race-based insults, but this was the first time that a White person had hurled a classist allegation against me. That was the end of an otherwise amusing friendship.

I befriended other more senior graduate students whose offices were located some distance from ours. Joe Smucker, who worked in industrial sociology, introduced me to a new world of his life as a Mennonite who had served as a conscientious objector in South Korea for 3 years, for which I admired him. His knowledge of world music and early protest songs increased my grasp of this genre of music. Another student from Poona in India, Hambir Phadtare, was one of the most gentle people I met. Although he was a demographer and our approaches to sociology differed considerably, as did our notions of "being Indian," he was good humored about my nontraditional behavior as a diasporic Indian.

During my stay in Michigan, I met Eqbal Ahmad, the brother of my friend and fellow student, Saghir Ahmad. He invited me to speak about political developments in South Africa at the University of Illinois, where he was teaching at the time. I was attracted to the broadness of his exposure: He was forced to relocate to Pakistan from India as a child, studied at Princeton, became fluent in French, and wrote a biography of Habib Bourguiba of Tunisia. Earlier he had lived in Algeria and worked on the labor movement there. During the Algerian war against the French, he joined Algeria's National Liberation Front (FLN) and was later arrested by the French in Paris. He was very different from the Muslims I encountered in my childhood. His views on Israel/Palestine, though very sober, as Edward Said mentions about him, nevertheless brought him into conflict with some Israelis. We stayed in touch after I returned to South Africa. He was a remarkably modest person for all his achievements and his wide circle of associates and friends, among them Frantz Fanon, Noam Chomsky, and Edward Said. Wherever I travel in the world, even today, well after his death in 1999, there is always someone who has heard of his passion for challenging injustice and violence against humanity. I will never forget his concern about my personal safety after I returned to South Africa and decided not to come back to the United States as he had encouraged me to do. He contacted the American consulate in Durban to see if I was safe, even offering to send me a ticket. His friends mattered.

Education in the United States, in contrast to my South African experiences, had a personally liberating influence. Identifying with the civil rights movement, participating in anti-Vietnam War discussions, and understanding student demonstrations in Berkeley exposed me to big questions both locally and internationally. Exposure to American daily realities, income disparities, and persistent racial inequalities for many longstanding minorities, quickly broke down the Hollywood myth, that all Americans enjoyed the glitzy affluent lifestyle portrayed in movies abroad. . At the same time, as I was leaving in 1965, the passage of the Immigration and Nationality Act, which banned immigration quotas of origin, heralded a new vision of what makes a person American. It opened up the past prioritizing of European ancestry as the only authentic American. No longer was race and ethnic origin a regulating feature. In so doing, America held out the promise of accessibility to the world without quotas. All of this, notwithstanding, internal poverty structures and the institutions that nurtured them remained slow-moving in many areas.

As an international student, teaching and learning styles at American universities opened up the world for me, though I sometimes considered viewpoints taken a little naive and lacking broader third-world exposure. I no longer felt constrained by "how" I spoke, which had inhibited communication in my earlier education. I experienced a sense of people willing to listen respectfully to what I had to say, to consider different opinions. I was expected to be knowledgeable about South Africa, and I tried to live up to these expectations.

In the large South African lecture halls during my undergraduate years, I had never once dared to raise a question. One's accent mattered, and even though I had been very carefully taught to mimic, it constrained the daring to question. There was always the fear that a superior colonial could "demolish" the question, and I would be left with no resources to retaliate. Of course, large classes and formal lecture setups inhibited participation, for starters. The small tutorial setups were equally horrifying for the eyeballing one-on-one and the lack of a real grasp of the abstract concepts with no hooks to hang them on from our daily lives. The resulting long silences terrified the instructor as much as it did us. Between educator and student there was a fundamental absence of trust. In the United States, the great value for personal growth, reiterated by many South African students fortunate to live abroad, was the opportunity to gain confidence away from one's country of origin. I'm sure the same applied to other international students living and learning outside their home countries.

Later, working in teacher education in Canada, I sensed immigrant children as second-language speakers often viewed themselves as "lesser" than English-first language speakers. It made me wonder about the effects that would result from a chance to visit the country of their parents' origin, where they saw people like themselves, in power, using their home languages in running a country. While this may have succeeded for immigrant minorities, what about the fate of indigenous native minorities for whom this alternative did not work?

CHAPTER 6

Teaching at a Tribal College

After I returned from the United States in 1965 with a master's degree in sociology and anthropology, the South African universities had all been not only racially segregated, but also ethnically divided. Previously my university education took place at a so-called open university, the University of Natal in Durban. We were taught by the same professors in racially segregated classes in the Non-European Section of the university. However, in 1959 under the euphemistically labeled Extension of University Education Act, Non-White students were excluded from entry into the previously "open" universities. Instead, separate universities were set up for Colored students at the University of the Western Cape and for Indians at the University College; for Africans, universities were further divided along ethnic lines: The University of the North was for Sotho, Venda, and Tsonga speakers; Fort Hare University for Xhosa speakers; and the University of Zululand for Zulu and Swazi speakers. The only university at which I could teach was the one designated specifically for Indians. It was situated on Salisbury Island in the Durban harbor and accessible either by ferry or a much longer drive around the Bluff. The buildings were army and navy barracks that were no longer in use. We had chosen to boycott participation in the government project of racially segregated education with an underlying curriculum aimed at retaining the specific culture of each group as defined by the state. We mocked those who had readily taken positions to work within the system earlier on when it was initiated. Alternative part-time educational arrangements had been set up for many years by the South African College of Higher Education (SACHED) offering students correspondence courses to avoid enrolling at these institutions. But as time went on, the viability of the alternative decreased. SACHED's part-time nature, the lack of a structured full-time alternative, and a limited choice of curricular offerings led to its declining enrollment. Wealthier parents sent their children abroad to study, while the poorer saw no alternative but to give in to the apartheid institution with the idea of making the best of what it had to offer. After all, in reality, our entire lives had been in different variations of segregated institutions. This was the climate I faced upon returning from my studies in the United States.

Initially resisting, I took on part-time teaching of English at a high school, which was the only option. But after a while friends and relatives asked me to reconsider, restrategize, and use what I had learned in the United States in my field of study to the advantage of students who had no other option than to attend these institutions. I was reminded that "The same government pays your salary as a teacher in a high school for Indians only, so what's the point of your resisting teaching sociology at university level in an institution segregated the same as all the others?" After some consideration, I reluctantly went to meet the rector of the University College, S. P. Olivier. My initial meeting can only be described as "cagey." After all, a person returning after studying in the United States could likely be a disturbing and disruptive addition in such an institution. "Why did you choose to study in the United States? Didn't you think you could get a better education here in South Africa?" Nothing more was said, other than a hypocritical smile and parting words of, "If any positions arise, we will let you know."

Several months passed. I heard nothing, nor did I expect to. As I had to commit to the school teaching appointment, I followed up with a phone call to arrange another appointment to see if the situation had changed. This time the rector retread previous "safe" conversational themes, but then during the course of our meeting, as if a change of heart occurred spontaneously, he said, "I think we may have found an opening to try you out." Olivier was known to be a stalwart of the Moral Rearmament Movement. Individuals committed to this approach made decisions on the basis of personal guidance from God. Though the movement initially aimed strongly at seeking social justice and transformation, it was suspicious of those actively involved politically as allied with communism. For us, it was difficult not to be politically engaged and enraged by the daily experience of apartheid.

So began my stint in a college designated for Indians only. Most of the teaching faculty were Afrikaans-speaking Whites, frequently former civil servants. One had to adapt to the fact that there was to be no social contact between the White and Non-White faculty. One had to know one's place in the racialized hierarchy. At teatime, the norm was to fetch one's tea from the staff room and either drink it alone or take the tea to one's own office. I chose to break this custom, lingered and stood there attempting to open conversations with limited success. In light of the unwelcoming atmosphere, many of us opted for having our own tea supplies in our offices. Toilets were labelled for White men, White women, Non-White men and Non-White women. On one occasion I quickly stepped inside a White women's toilet to adjust a slip that was showing under my skirt. The next day the rector's secretary called to "correct" me on the use of the wrong toilet! I was so incensed by the situation that I refused to explain my hurried entry into the White women's toilet. I was reminded of a common tale told of a White priest entering a church for Whites only. Upon finding an African cleaner inside, he asked him, "Are you sure you were not praying in the church?"

Contrary to existing conventions of no social contacts with White faculty, I befriended a liberal Afrikaans-speaking fellow lecturer who lived not far from my home. She often rode home with me on days when I drove my VW Beetle to work, and one day we arranged to play tennis on campus with two other colleagues after classes. Within a day, I received a notice from the rector's office that the tennis courts were reserved for the exclusive use of White faculty on Mondays, Wednesdays, and Fridays and for Non-White faculty on Tuesdays and Thursdays.

That effectively ended our integrated matches. White faculty were invited to social events in the evenings from which Non-White faculty were excluded. A thoughtful, guilt-ridden Afrikaner social work colleague, Hermann Rocher, tried to make up for this exclusion by inviting me to lunch at his home in the company of his very politically aware wife, on the day preceding the evening events. I appreciated his recognition of the injustice and attempting to make amends, when all others turned a blind eye to the exclusion of those they were entrusted to work with.

Many Afrikaans-speaking colleagues were placed in these positions, with lesser academic qualifications, as part of their promotion from the civil service. They were also paid an additional stipend for the "hardship" endured in teaching "others" in these isolated ethnic campuses. Students complained about the quality of instruction offered by some of these new appointees, whose English fluency was limited and who in some instances dictated notes verbatim from the correspondence course outlines of the University of South Africa (UNISA).

There was absolutely no social contact between teaching faculty in a university where they were expected to know the population they were teaching, and whose "culture" they were expected to be furthering. I experienced the fear of contact in a young male colleague with whom I had to share the grading of some questions on student examination papers. When I went to his office to collect these, he stood up in fright, opened the door of his office totally, and placed a chair to ensure it would remain open, and then quickly handed me the papers, so that there could be no mistaking of inappropriate contact between us. Needless to say I found the assumption presumptuous.

There were dress codes that laundered all dangers of stimulating sexual fantasies. Women faculty were not allowed to wear open-toed sandals and were required to be "appropriately" dressed. I refused to wear a sari, which would have conformed to their idea of culturally appropriate dress. What would have irritated me was the "respect" I would have received from a racist institution for cultural conformity and for "identifying with my community" thereby "knowing my place." At the same time, I sensed an ambivalence among White colleagues there who were uncomfortable with too much "difference" and, in fact, preferred the assimilated "other" who knew their place.

This tenuous contact between Whites and Non-Whites was not only due to the nature of this apartheid institution; I believe it was endemic at so many levels in South African society. For instance, during my time at the Stellenbosch Institute of Advanced Study (STIAS) decades later after the formal end of apartheid, I met a well-respected Afrikaans-speaking poet and her artist husband who had lived in Durban for 6 years and taught at the University of Durban–Westville, the integrated successor of the tribal college on Salisbury Island. They mentioned casually that during this time they had not made a single social contact with any Indian or African person, neither student nor colleagues, attributing this to the "social climate." What this told me was that there were deeply internalized group-specific "comfort zones" that prevailed. I asked myself what would make it possible for an otherwise friendly liberal White Afrikaans-speaking couple to live and teach predominantly

Indian and African students in another province for 6 years and not make a single social contact with either colleagues or students? Could it be because those colleagues and students were not Afrikaans-speaking? Why were they not curious to step outside these comfort zones to meet "the other"?

An instance in my parents' experience highlighted the remnants of socially appropriate contact in different situations. They had downsized from their home, after apartheid laws were changing, and bought an apartment in a racially integrated block on the waterfront in Durban. They befriended a liberal Afrikaans-speaking couple from the Boland in the Cape. My mother and this politically progressive, elegant, hypochondriacal woman developed very warm relations with each other. It had to always be at her apartment since she had mobility issues making visiting easier in her apartment. They met often for coffee and sharing family stories. Occasionally, her husband would drop by at my parents' flat, and the men had a whiskey together. All this said and done, I recall my mother telling me that my father had mentioned how strange it was that the same man who was so friendly with them in private, would never speak to him at the tenants' meetings when they were all together. He avoided revealing that they knew each other socially. This was not at all unusual in South Africa. I too had experienced this with colleagues where social conventions guided association. A White Natal businessman, who customarily kissed me when he welcomed us in his home, behaved very formally in the presence of his fellow White businessmen at a public event at their club, where he formally shook my hand to greet us.

Another prominent White businessman, who had sought Heribert's help in drafting a policy document, offered us their guest cottage on the Natal coast, which was right beside theirs. All the necessities to make the stay comfortable were generously provided, but they never dropped in or invited us to visit them during our stay. There were various possible explanations: to give us privacy and space? To avoid breaking down the social code of who socializes with whom? An Indian woman married to a White man would break the social code, as well as the operating racial hierarchy of master and servant (most of their employees were Indian), to which they were accustomed. Customary behavior of the race-based kind still persists even in post-Mandela South Africa. Most restaurants in central Cape Town have either an exclusively or predominantly White or Black clientele. Could it be driven by different tastes in food and music, different personal comfort zones, or economic factors?

But I have digressed.

For the most part, my teaching career at University College went smoothly, as far as I could tell. There were signs, however, that all was not well. On a day when I had no classes to teach and chose to work at home instead of driving all the way to the campus, the department head reported this as absence, and my salary was reduced for that day. A department head monitoring whether a colleague was working in her office or not on a nonteaching day indicated the frost was setting in.

Sometime after, on September 19, 1967, I was requested to appear at a meeting of the Council to be held in Pretoria to assess my experiences over the past

18 months on a temporary contract, apparently to shift it into a permanent lectureship. So I traveled all the way there by car to be on time for the meeting. It necessitated an overnight stay, and since there were no hotels for Non-Whites at the time, I stayed with friends of my parents. I should have billed the Council for travel expenses and overnight costs, but so unskilled was I in asserting these rights at the time, that I left financial matters unaddressed. The meeting took place at the Department of Indian Affairs in Pretoria. Although scheduled for 2:50 p.m., I was not called in until 4 p.m. Six Afrikaner professors were seated in a very formal room with dark green leather-covered chairs. An administrative assistant at the end of the table recorded the session. Immediately after the meeting, I too made detailed notes of the questions asked and my replies, from which I now quote. It was indeed a formal interrogation.

The questions went as follows: "You have taught at UCD for the past year. How do you feel about the establishment of a separate university for this community? Would you give us a brief statement of your experiences at the college—your attitude . . . before you came here and now that you have been there?" My answer was that I had essentially enjoyed working with the students I taught. It was for me a new kind of challenge, different from the students with whom I had worked in the United States. I attempted to make my teaching relevant to the lives of the students I taught locally, gradually broadening out to look at societal and international problems. Another question: "You talk of Indian South Africans; . . . are they different from any other kind of Indians? I answered that they constituted a new kind of mixture given that they were nurtured in a different environment. "How can you hold yourself up as an expert on India? Have you ever been there?" I replied that I had visited India once for 6 weeks, but I was familiar with international studies about the Indian diaspora. I was accused of making judgements on the basis of a short visit, and how could I call myself a sociologist with such a small window of contact. I attempted to cite other sources of my knowledge of India without much success. Then the topic changed with a question from my department head, G. K. Engelbrecht, about the relevance of Durkheim and his impact on a study called *The Human Group* by Homans. This was quickly followed with my impending visit to Germany, scholarships for which I had applied, and "Why Germany?" My response was that I have always been interested in German sociological theory and have been taking German language lessons over the past 6 months to be able to read the original texts. This answer seemed to arouse an emotional response from almost all of those present. Notes were passed. (The note probably mentioned: "Applied for a German scholarship and has a German boyfriend!") Next question: "You know Indians have now been accepted as an integral part of South Africa; why is it that you have been studying German and do not know Afrikaans?" Even before I had a chance to address the previous one: "Do you accept the situation in South Africa?" I replied that I live in this country and by virtue of this have no choice but to accept the situation. This angered those present, and one person said that I should never have been on the campus in the first place. But in an attempt to placate the situation, the rector pointed out that this was a democratic country.

Then they asked: "Do you have any questions?" I asked what they envisaged the position of Indians to be within the foreseeable future? Engelbrecht responded, "They will become more Westernized!" Upon which the rector immediately countered, "No, they will have to move in the other direction . . . they will have to maintain their own identity . . . and in so doing play an important part in world affairs, in the Middle East and India—that is the answer to your question!" Clearly two senior figures at the same institution had different views of their mission. One further question came: "Would you say separate education is a good thing and has been accepted by South African Indians?" My response did not help. I said that initially we were all against the establishment of a separate institution, our major fear among others was losing contact with other groups in our society and a lowering of academic standards. One person interjected with a request for clarification about what kind of contact I was referring to, social or academic? To which I warily responded "academic," knowing full well that social contact was totally unacceptable in their worldview. As to the measure of acceptance of the institution of separate universities for each group, I answered that its success could only be measured if Indians had the choice of attending either the "open" university or their own "Indian" university. The knee-jerk response of the rector was that this was an "a posteriori" argument and totally unacceptable, as only 20% of students would have come if there were a choice. Again, the topic changed: As a sociologist what do you think is the birthrate of Indians in South Africa? How would you propose to reduce the birthrate? When you teach sociology, which theorists do you offer students? Why do you include Marx among the texts you choose for your students to read? At the very end, it became clear to me that they had information I had not given them formally, namely, that I had applied to the German Academic Exchange Service (DAAD) for a fellowship in the following year. I can only say the atmosphere was a hostile one. Nothing more transpired until later that year.

In a private meeting at 7:00 a.m. in late November 1967, with the rector of University College, S. P. Olivier, I was informed that "for reasons beyond my control, I will have to terminate your services at the end of this year." When asked for the grounds of the termination, and no answer was forthcoming other than that there were forces beyond his control that required him to do it, my final words to him were, "Could you tell me, how you as the head of an academic institution feel about a dismissal, as you mention, on nonacademic grounds?" His answer was, "Miss Moodley, the Lord opens new paths where old ones close." Years later, shortly before he passed away, he requested a visit with my sister and her husband in Durban to ask for forgiveness for his collaborative role in my unjust dismissal. This lay heavily on his conscience.

Despite the anger, the powerlessness, the finality of closing options to employment in South Africa, since the Security Branch had declared me a persona non grata, I needed to know what was on file. One Indian Special Branch investigator, Sergeant Nayagar, had come to my home soon after I returned from the United States, but mainly asked whom I had met and what I had published abroad. Over the years, the unanswered question for me was, what precisely were "the forces beyond" the rector's control? No answers were forthcoming until about 40 years later.

I was in Cape Town and invited to a book launch at the residence of the British High Commissioner to South Africa in Bishop's Court, hosted by the visiting former British High Commissioner, Robin Renwick. On that occasion I noticed a familiar face from the past, an Afrikaans-speaking philosophy professor, Willie Esterhuyse, who was on the faculty of the University College during my time there. I introduced myself. "You may not remember me. We were both colleagues on Salisbury Island, at University College. But in those days the philosophers didn't talk to the sociologists!" Being in a convivial mood, sipping a glass of wine, he replied, "Of course I remember you. I saved you from being arrested! I can even give you the name of the security policeman who tipped me off and I told him to leave you alone!"

I was in a state of shock and relief. It was the first time someone had acknowledged what had happened to me and had some valuable information. Clearly, this was not the place to get those details, but he promised to arrange an occasion to talk about it. I gave him my card, but nothing ensued from this. On my next visit to Cape Town, I managed to reach him and arranged a lunch meeting in Stellenbosch at the Volkskombuis restaurant. At this cordial lunch, he began by telling me that when he was teaching at University College, he often preached on the weekend at the local Dutch Reformed Church. He was not an ordained minister, he said, but thought it important to raise consciousness. One day, a man came up to him and said how much his sermon had made him think, and it opened his mind. Esterhuyse asked him what he did for a living, to which he replied that he had a furniture store. Esterhuyse responded saying this was good to know and if he needed stuff he would contact him. The next evening, the man knocked on the door of Esterhuyses's home and asked if he could speak to him. He then confessed that he had lied to him: The furniture store was only a foil for his real work as a security policeman. He said he wanted to give Esterhuyse a heads-up on important news that was about to break. In the next few days they were about to arrest one of his colleagues at the university. That was me! Esterhuyse apparently asked him not to do that and, in his words, to "leave her alone." He never told me what the offense was for which I was about to be arrested. I was not told to be careful, which a caring colleague might have done. He couldn't give me the name of the agent as he had promised, saying that he had died.

In the meantime, in a curious turn of events, Esterhuyse had befriended Thabo Mbeki, or vice versa, who was to succeed Mandela as President. In 1988–1989 Esterhuyse played a role as go-between for the security establishment in South Africa and the ANC in London (see Esterhuyse, 2012). Even a Hollywood movie, *Endgame,* portrayed the philosopher as the main actor strolling in deep thought around Stellenbosch as mediator and enabler of liberation. How Mbeki came to choose Esterhuyse as his contact to the Afrikaner establishment is not clear to me. A talk with the security policeman who threatened to arrest me resulted in his protection of someone he did not even know personally, much to his credit. Many questions came to mind: Why did he do it? Would it not have been important to find out what I had done that he was protecting me from? Could he have protected me by giving me a tip-off? Now, decades later over lunch that day, he mentioned that the campus had been "teeming with security people," obviously in search of activists and potential agitators. All along I had suspected security branch surveillance, but I wondered how he had come to know this?

The DAAD had communicated privately that I had been granted a fellowship to visit Germany in 1968 on a 6-month academic exchange, and that all that remained was for them to get government clearance. Subsequently, they communicated that unfortunately they had to withdraw their offer on the grounds that they were not able to receive South African government approval for me. I challenged them about who they were seeking to select with a requirement of government permission. Their disproportionate allocation of 13 fellowships—10 for Whites and 1 each for Africans, Indians, and Coloreds—was grossly unfair. The DAAD was embarrassed. I received their promise that they would honor their original offer, and that I should book my flight to arrive in Germany as soon as it was convenient for me. They included special privileges such as unlimited entry to the Berlin Philharmonic and Opera.

I had a meeting in Bonn with the DAAD director at the time, Hubertus Scheibe, and to their credit, the DAAD listened and noted the problems with their procedures and subsequently modified their practices. One was reminded of the ignorance with which foreign governments shaped their policies for South Africa. Nor was the DAAD alone in this. Many foreign agencies at the time unquestioningly collaborated with those in power in the apartheid state as if this were the only legitimate way to proceed and they had no choice.

In retrospect, the years I spent working at this apartheid institution raised some serious doubts about the assumptions made in the social science literature on intergroup relations.

We had been led to believe in the power of equal status contact in building positive bonds between people. My experiences during this period proved otherwise. The salience of the question in my earlier interview about whether I meant "academic contact" or "social contact" illustrated the fact that in a deeply racist society, and despite a shared project of teaching, norms about appropriate interracial contact were so entrenched in socialization and reinforced by state policies that normal contact between individuals across these lines was rendered impossible.

CHAPTER 7

An Enduring Friendship

I first met Heribert in 1966, ironically in the forbidden halls of the apartheid institution established for Indians on Salisbury Island, Durban. One might say it was an arranged marriage, introduced unwittingly by G. K. Engelbrecht, my department head. Flattered by the visit of a German sociologist who wished to learn about South Africa, it was suggested that the visitor speak to my class on Sociological Theory. And so it all began.

Politically conscious people of my age at that time had been raised to be deeply suspicious of visitors to such apartheid institutions. Immediately, I had a predisposition to be highly skeptical of our visitor. Our role as opponents of the system was to utilize every opportunity to "inform" foreigners to counteract the official lines to which they may have been exposed. With this is mind, I agreed to postpone my own lecture, not that I had much choice after being "asked" in an authoritarian system by a superior, who, intent on showing off his German fluency, even offered to introduce the speaker in German. I listened carefully to the talk. When the visitor referred to leftist sources and theorists, particularly *The Authoritarian Personality* by his own PhD supervisor, Theodor Adorno et al., my interest perked. Those unfamiliar with these radical sources were unable to detect the critical thread in this speech, and its implicit application to the local situation.

The visitor was to be entertained, but when a venue was explored, what should have been common knowledge in an apartheid country came as a surprise to the head of department who, like most White South Africans, knew little of everyday apartheid in practice, since they never socialized out of their own White enclaves. The White restaurants wouldn't accept a "mixed' group, the one Indian restaurant was not open in the evenings, the wife of the department head would never entertain a "Non-White" person in their home, and so I suggested that they come to my parental home. This provided a way out, and Engelbrecht offered to bring a bottle of Harveys Bristol Sherry, of which he was very proud. I didn't know much about wine in those days and how Germans weren't great fans of sweet wine, such as sherry. Besides, in Indian homes, alcohol was not a customary offering. And so they arrived: Two of my colleagues who were social work lecturers, Engelbrecht, and the visitor from Germany. Everyone sipped sherry feverishly to compensate for the awkwardness of the situation. Firstly, we were socializing in the presence of the head of department, uncustomary in an authoritarian society. Moreover, South Africans of all shades stand in awe of scholars from "overseas," and the presence of a German visiting academic intimidated them. Furthermore, it was the first time my Afrikaner colleagues had been in a multiracial social setting, in an Indian home to boot. And so the discussion proceeded very gingerly, beginning with Germany and the beauty of South Africa. The visitor was able to ask a few questions about the challenges faced with such vast inequality between groups. And after all the meandering talk, finally the point was made by the department head about how well South Africa was doing compared to the rest of Africa. And this went on, albeit haltingly, for some time. One has to keep in mind the authoritarian nature of collegial relations. It was also customary to avoid political topics with superiors, let alone in the presence of a Non-White, so there was a general agreement on the positive state of developments in South Africa.

At some point, unable to resist any longer, I had to come in with, "I'm not sure if we are talking about the same country. . . . This very home, owned by my parents for many years, has to be vacated under the Group Areas Act, for the exclusive occupation of White people. And all this under the umbrella of the Department of Community Development." Well, there was an uncomfortable silence, and politely the department head made some noises about how unfortunate this was, and it shouldn't have happened. And after a few more pleasantries, the evening came to an end. Our guest was invited to be driven home by my colleagues, but he declined, saying it wasn't necessary and he would be getting a ride home a little later.

Once they had all left, although I didn't know Heribert at all, we both burst into a bout of the most relieved laughter that showed the stress we had experienced from this awkward meeting. In this moment a shared unspoken understanding opened between us: where "we" stood as opposed to "them." He was concerned about the consequences of my outspokenness in the presence of an outsider, and publicly challenging the views of my superior. And so began a friendship, although, already unspoken, it was a little more than that.

Heribert asked whether I would show him a bit of the Indian settlements around Durban, and I agreed to drive him there in my VW the following day. We talked about his interest in studying the "Nazis of South Africa," an analogy he subsequently revised in his book *Modernizing Racial Domination* (1971); my work in the United States; and the interest I had in the work of Max Weber. He encouraged me to apply for a scholarship to study in Germany and recommended that I contact the DAAD, the German academic exchange program. And then he had to continue his South African tour with the group with whom he had come to South Africa. Soon after that, I left for India on a long-arranged 1-month visit with my parents. When I came back, to my great surprise, Heribert had decided to return to South Africa. He had arranged a visiting 1-year position teaching sociology at the University of Natal.

During this year I got to know him better. He was a frequent visitor in our home, and I introduced him to the American consular people I had come to know after my return from the United States, and many other friends. I was skeptical about the impressions he had been able to gain from interviews with Afrikaners in Pretoria who had also been the hosts of the three-person German research group. He was able to detect signs of pragmatism in their approach to apartheid, and a willingness to change. He listened to viewpoints I had been programmed to dismiss as "window dressing" and "empty rhetoric." In hindsight he was proven to have been right by the negotiated settlement 3 decades later. Another area of my skepticism was about the combination of critical theory with psychoanalytic reasoning. My sociological education led me to distance myself from psychological perspectives, especially Freud. But with time, I came to rethink this, although I continue to use this combination cautiously.

Our relationship had grown in intensity; the initial attraction flowered into deeper feelings for one another. We shared so much at so many levels. However, to avoid arrest under the Immorality Act, we had always to be careful never to be alone in a car or in his apartment. One could be arrested with "having the intent to commit an immoral act." The stigma of being arrested under the Immorality Act would have been painful to my family and would have resulted in much ugly publicity and imprisonment. We were justifiably scared by the much-publicized, revolting reporting of police peering from the trees beside a bedroom of the home of John Blacking, a British ethnomusicologist, and capturing his relationship with an Indian woman, Zureena Desai, leading to their arrest. After prosecution, they left Africa together, later married, and settled in Belfast. The irony of the situation was that even my community would have viewed this as inappropriate behavior for an Indian woman from a respectable family—the political underpinnings of this forbidding legislation was lost on them. Without explicitly discussing this, Heribert and I were always mindful of the implications and agreed on seeing each other only in safe settings. Only once did we travel to Mozambique in the company of friends to stay with the mother of a Portuguese friend, which gave us a reprieve from the agonizing repressive conditions under which we loved each other secretly. Needless to say, the head of my department once alluded to difficulty we had at the border, slyly and disapprovingly indicating to me that he was aware of us traveling to Mozambique and that security police had information he was privy to. In retrospect, I should have paid more attention to this lead since it ultimately led to consequences for my employment.

During that year, Heribert, without explicitly saying so, was planning my future very carefully, step by step. He arranged for me to take German language lessons with an instructor teaching the course at the University of Natal, with the apparent aim of facilitating my application for the DAAD fellowship. He went to much trouble to help me in filling out the forms and even sat there typing with two fingers on an old clunky typewriter. Needless to say, the relationship was growing under the most trying of circumstances. After my evening lecture, I often drove by Heribert's apartment block and would have given anything to stop by and see him, but knowing how dangerous this could be, I resisted. We hesitated to call each other fearing that our phone lines were tapped. It could have been a chaperoned courtship, always in the presence of others, but no affection could be shown. However, this was not unusual for Indian women at the time, who customarily lived at home prior to being married. His boldest move, unknown to me, was to send a touristic postcard to his mother in Germany with three bare-breasted Black women, with his accompanying text, "Guess which of the three will be your daughter-in-law?" This devout Catholic lady must have had the shock of her life about her much-loved errant son's future.

After some time, Heribert was getting quite irritated with the situation and of our separated lives. To be in love with someone one could never spontaneously visit, was the hardest thing to endure for both of us. Furthermore, we realized there were forces at work to get us into a situation where we would be violating the law by being alone with each other. I would receive harassing anonymous phone calls from aggressive White males, clearly security police agents, on my home phone, inviting me to go out with them. When I asked who was speaking, the response was, "I met you at a party!" When asked again for the name, the response was, "I can't tell you because I'm White!" When I tried to end the call with, "I don't know you and don't want to hear from you," I received the most horrible vulgar sexual expletives imaginable before they hung up. They were clearly frustrated at not being able to arrest Heribert and me violating the law, so they were trying to set me up. I felt unclean and violated. I had to keep all of this to myself and did not mention this either to Heribert or my parents. I could not bear to repeat what was said and I did not wish to terrify the whole family with whom I lived. Throughout, my parents were amazing in never making me fearful of the dangers I might face. They trusted my judgement completely. One day Heribert came to visit our home and told me how difficult it was for him to function with all these constraints, and asked whether I would consider leaving with him. Despite how much I loved him, how much we shared the same ideals and interests, this was a huge question for me. How does one leave the familiar to go to the unknown? South Africa was "home," after all. What would I do in a new situation with unfettered freedom and a fear that I might never be able to return if my passport expired? I had the security of a job, despite the constraints of its pro-apartheid administration. I loved teaching where I could make a difference. I said I needed time.

Many things come to mind about how Heribert coped with the situation during that period. He led a one-man boycott, refusing to go to any venue that was reserved for Whites only. At least I still had the contact of family and community. Other than being at the university, he spent most of his time alone, conducting research and reading on South Africa. Occasionally, he insisted on inviting my entire family out to Whites-only restaurants, only to break the rules. He played up the role of his being a foreigner from Germany who wanted to take this family out for dinner, and on a few occasions the manager at bigger hotels reneged so as not to risk negative publicity. The Indian waiters muttered to each other in hushed voices, "Let's serve them well!" And we were again a curiosity to other patrons. I thought then how ironic it was that an outsider had to come to our country to "allow" us to have the "privilege" of eating in a Whites-only establishment in my very own country.

One evening, Heribert invited us all to his apartment on the Esplanade, where he would prepare a European meal for us. The first course was escargot, then a steak, which emerged from a smoke-filled kitchen because, as a man with few culinary skills, he grilled the steaks without a tray beneath to catch the dripping fat. It was amazing that the kitchen didn't catch on fire. Then came the salad and a dessert. By the end of the meal, which took some time, my father was half asleep at the table. My mother was on her best behavior by even trying the escargot because with her fine palette, she liked the garlic butter sauce and the French bread. They even nibbled politely on the steak, though customarily Hindu families never eat beef! And so the evening proceeded, ending on a fine note of how capable a cook our friend was. As I was to learn subsequently, it was a one-off show, never to be repeated during a marriage of several decades!

Heribert was immensely thoughtful of others, and liked nothing more than to help someone with an interest in learning. In our home we had taken on the responsibility of caring for the son of an African woman who worked for us. We taught him all the school skills he needed and read stories with him, and he simply hung out with us. Seeing this, one day Heribert gave him a gift of a little portable radio, so that he could hear the news and become better informed. Another way Heribert contributed to our family was to offer his services to help with the building of a retaining wall in the garden. He showed his physical prowess in such a way that the African gardeners said to each other in Zulu: "Aye, I've never seen a *Mulungu* (White man) work like us!"

Heribert's intellectual curiosity was always testing new hypotheses about South African society. No conversation was just idle, and it helped that he had a wonderful sense of humor. We talked about what we had read, what new books were published, how we interpreted political happenings, and what our thoughts were on potential future scenarios: This sharing sustained our virtually imprisoned existence.

Heribert was also becoming quite comfortable with the incessant socializing in Indian family life. Originating from a traditional German family where there was close three-generational contact, the transition seemed smooth, and the openness of the Indian kitchen ready to offer meals to any visitor without much notice was something that he admired. This differed considerably, I was to learn, from the formality of dinner invitations characteristic of German social life where everything had to be perfect and there were often more dishes and cutlery than there was food on the well-set table. There were some culture shocks when we attended Indian weddings and people were served beautiful vegetarian meals on banana leaves. It was customary with such large gatherings that people used their fingers to eat the meal. As someone who had his fingers slapped as a child for not using his cutlery, he had to learn that eating with one's fingers has a certain decorum as well, and involved fingertip skills! Another surprise for him was that alcohol was served to the men only, away from public view, often in a bedroom or secluded lounge.

We attended the public funeral of Nobel laureate Chief Albert Luthuli in Eshowe. ANC and SACP flags fluttered in the wind openly. Observing this, Heribert remarked that this would not have been possible in the totalitarian Nazi system without deadly repercussions for the dissenters. It was an emotional experience to hear Alan Paton's eulogy translated into powerful Zulu. He was a master at evoking the right images, and the crowds' response in unison was moving and provided evidence that he had touched them. Alan Paton invited us to visit him at his home, and daring to drive out together alone in my Beetle, we spent an afternoon in conversation with him, returning during a strong hailstorm which may have also spared us police surveillance.

Our circle of academic friends had expanded to Tony Mathews, from the Law Department, psychologist Ronald Albino, sociologist Lawrie Schlemmer, and above all, Jairam Reddy, who played a significant role as leader in the country's academic institutions. The American consul, John Savage, always on the lookout for political stories to report back, and supportive of the political opposition, provided many opportunities for socializing at his home. Our regular enjoyable tennis doubles matches on Sunday mornings on the University of Natal tennis courts were however brought to an abrupt end. Players included Heribert, Jairam Reddy, John Savage, and myself. Heribert received a written reprimand from the then Vice Chancellor of the University of Natal, Owen Horwood, notifying him that interracial sport was not permitted on university premises under the Group Areas Act.

On one occasion we were invited to dinner at the Bellair home of Rick Turner, a cult figure on campus and activist philosopher, who wrote *The Eye of the Needle: Towards Participatory Democracy in South Africa* (1972). To our embarrassment we arrived a day earlier through some misunderstanding. Being the unconventional person he was, Rick insisted we stay and prepared an improvised meal with his partner, Fowzia Fischer, while having memorable conversations. Tragically, Rick was assassinated in 1978 by an apartheid agent, shot through the window of his home, and died in the arms of his 13-year-old daughter.

Heribert's main sponsor, Hamish Dickie-Clarke, then head of the Sociology Department, had previously been my formidable instructor. He was incapable of engaging his students to participate in his tutorials. He simply didn't know what to do when students were not forthcoming in keeping a discussion going. We had difficulty talking about ideas in the abstract. The textbook he assigned was *The Human Group* by G. C. Homans, and even today I can reaffirm this as the most boring choice guaranteed to turn students off the subject. This was a classical example of how the nonconvergence of White and Indian worlds led to the lack of a shared universe of meaning in their everyday worlds. A meaningful dialogue begins by asking the right questions. To do this, one has to understand the worlds of those we seek to reach. Upon Heribert's initiation, Hamish invited me to join them for dinner at his home one evening. He insisted on picking me up from my home to ensure Heribert and I would not be driving together. Only much later did Heribert mention that Hamish had gently counseled him about what he considered were real cultural differences between us and that he should be aware of the likely problems with such relationships.

As things developed, Heribert asked me if I would write a chapter for a book he was editing. Fatima Meer, a sociologist and political activist, was also asked to write a chapter. It was for me and for Fatima, as she mentioned to me, the first time anyone had thought we had anything worthwhile to say that was publishable. This was when I wrote a piece titled "The Dialectic of Higher Education for the Colonized," which looked at the unintended politicizing consequences of separate institutions of higher learning for the various Non-White groups. A few years later, Steve Biko and Rick Turner used it for the conscientization of students. The writing of this piece became an important turning point in my life, as it did for Fatima Meer as well.

Unbeknownst to me, Heribert had sought the approval of my parents to marry me. My father apparently responded in a nontraditional way, that Heribert would have to ask me! When this was all subtly resolved, and it became clear that I was to leave for Germany, Heribert wanted to honor my parents by formally conducting an engagement ceremony in our home. The question was, how does one purchase an engagement ring together where we can both agree on the choice. If we went to a store, we would arouse suspicion about an immoral union. My father had a friend who was a trusted diamond dealer, who came to the house to show what he had to offer, since this visitor wanted to buy a stone to take back to Germany. I was not in the room to avoid suspicion. The choice was made and afterward taken to our goldsmith by me, to make the simplest setting for the occasion.

Thus it happened that one afternoon before I left for Germany, my mother and father and sisters, having drawn all the curtains in the living room, lit the prayer lamp and with a simple prayer, my parents blessed us and the symbol of the ring, which Heribert put on my finger. Of all times, that was when the doorbell rang! We quickly dispersed, removing any remaining signs of the ceremony. Our old cook and her daughter, whom we had not seen for years, were just dropping by for a Sunday visit. I quickly transferred the ring from the third finger of my left hand to my little pinky finger, and offered to make the tea, while Heribert disappeared into another part of the house.

A week later, Heribert left ahead of me for interviews in Johannesburg, so that we would not be seen flying together from Durban. So I bid farewell on my own from Durban. Before I left, my father, characteristically the caring romantic person, put into my hands an open return ticket from Frankfurt to Durban, traveler's checks to cover my expenses, and a pair of diamond earrings he had bought for me, telling me that I could have them reset to my preferred style. To this day, I have kept those as he gave them to me, as one of the most endearing memories of a thoughtful loving father.

Decades later, after all the bonding experiences Heribert and I have lived through, we have grown together inextricably. It is rare that two people from such different beginnings can embrace each other's families as their own, can share similar work interests, read similar texts and enjoy decoding them, write together, and offer sound critique coming from well-grounded perspectives. It has even come to the uncanny point sometimes that we can accurately anticipate what the other is thinking!

Does this mean there are no differences of opinion? Hardly. But it does mean we have learned to speak frankly and openly to voice these and hold our own until we can find a place of mutual acceptance and rethinking. I am always mindful of Archbishop Desmond Tutu's father's advice to him: "Lower your voice and sharpen your argument!" I feel fortunate to have met a person with such a sometimes annoying capacity for lowered voice, integrity, and respect. It reminds me of the seventh vow of our wedding service: "You will always be my best friend."

(*text continues on page 84*)

Moodley family photo, before my youngest sister was born.

A photo of me taken by daughter, Kanya, at her graduation from Oxford.

My daughters Kanya and Maya at Maya's graduation from Stanford.

My sisters and I with our mother, on the occasion of my mother's 100th birthday.

Above: Heribert and I in conversation on campus, 1979.
Below: Our Indian wedding ceremony in Frankfurt, conducted by my mother, Amartham.

The growth of the family enterprise: Crystal Ice Cream with delivery vans.

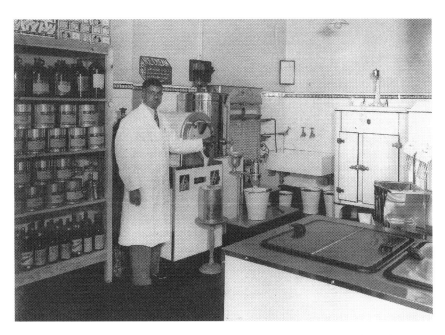

Uncle KR in his pristine "factory," using self-taught skills in making and marketing ice cream.

A view of the Art Deco style milk bar in Crystal Cafe, the first family business.

The family signs a contract with Shell Company to open Atlas Garage. Uncle KR, Uncle Vadivel, and Grandmother bless the enterprise.

Above: Percy Moodley, scratch golfer.
Below: Percy and Amartham at home in their eighties.

CHAPTER 8

Germany

Cultural, Linguistic, and Ideological Border Crossings

I arrived in Frankfurt Germany in late 1967 as a recipient of a DAAD fellowship, and I was to spend the first 4 months taking a German language course at the Goethe Institute in Berlin for 4 hours daily. My first exposure to the family of Heribert was in Dietesheim, 20 kilometers east of Frankfurt. With minimal German language, it still amazes me how one can communicate when there is goodwill on all sides. No knowledge of cultural differences might well have been an asset as we were simply thrown into each other's company to relate as human beings on the trivia of daily life. All we needed was an openness and flexibility to learn about each other's preferences as everyday life unfolded. This was all about learning in context. They were a harmonious family of three generations all living under one roof in separate suites on different floors. Heribert's father had not returned home from the Russian front, and his father's younger brother only miraculously returned from a Russian prison in 1956. A third brother, a theology professor at the University of Mainz, took on the role of Heribert's father in the hope that he would follow his footsteps into the clergy. The deeply Catholic aunts and mother not only had to deal with an agnostic son who had distanced himself from the church, but with an Indian non-Catholic "heathen"—in their view. Despite all these differences, I was received with warm affection. It reminded me of traditional Indian family life, although the German family had a better, more sustainable plan, with separate kitchens and more individual independence within an otherwise integrated togetherness. They had an unusual sense of humor, which came through in all the bantering between them. I felt very welcome not only by the immediate family but by the extended family and people in the neighborhood, which Heribert called "a village." It was very different from my notion of a village.

The streets and houses were meticulously clean and well cared for. Practically every house had cut flowers in vases or potted orchids on windowsills, carefully placed between lace curtains drawn open and tied on each side. Little specialty stores included a beautiful florist that served the steady market for flowers for all purposes: to celebrate an event, to take to friends one was visiting, and to take to the graveyard to honor the memory of a family member. There was also a hairdressing salon, where one could hear the latest gossip; a butchery, which sold fine sliced meats and sauces; a pharmacy; a bakery, producing fine crusty bread rolls and loaves of rye and other dark breads; an electrical store for small appliances; a shoe store; and a little grocery store, which sold cheeses, milk, and yogurt. The grocery store was run by an older woman who knew the history of every customer's family and remembered their names. What struck me was the meticulousness of every operation. The windows were cleaned daily; food was painstakingly, aesthetically arranged; and flowers were wrapped artistically in a way I'd never seen before. Every customer entered with the same greeting, "guten tag," and left with "auf wiedersehen." "Bitte" and "dankeschoen" frequently punctuated customers' visits. The one supermarket with super-efficient cashiers shoved customers' purchases at breakneck speed to the side after entering their prices on the cash register. If one stood there waiting for the purchases to be packed, one was in for a rude surprise. Customers were expected to quickly pack their own goods to make room for the next customer and were glared at for causing a delay. Clearly, the prescribed "modus operandi" made for quick, clear ordering and an admirable systematized packing style, the efficiency and likes of which I had never experienced before. Most people brought their own bags in with which to pack their purchases, so answered "no" when asked if they needed a plastic bag. Already then, there was careful, environmentally conscious use of plastics. From this I learned elementary lessons in how the stranger or newcomer without language skills comes to cope in such a regulated society. Exoticism and curiosity value of the newcomer is only part of the story.

When I didn't understand what Heribert's mother was saying, she simply raised her voice and repeated slowly. I am not sure what she thought of my capacity to learn. They spoke a Hessisches dialect, and the little German I knew on my arrival at Dietesheim was what I had learned at the University of Natal. Some of the course content, I subsequently discovered, provided totally erroneous real-life information. One unforgettable sentence, because it elicited such peals of laughter from Germans, was, "Aber Sonntags kocht mein Mann" (but on Sundays my husband cooks). The laughter seemed to mean "dream on!" The German course that I subsequently took in Berlin was in what they called "Hochdeutsch" (high German) with a Berlin accent, which I found easier to grasp than Hessisch. Rural or regional accents and dialects, particularly Bavarian, are not necessarily frowned upon, yet the family switched code from the local Hessisch to accommodate me. I was exempt from accusations of arrogance, usually associated with the use of Hochdeutsch in this area. In fact, the family was absolutely encouraging when I tried out my German. One comment was, "You have only been here a short time and you speak accent-free German, and look at these Italians who can only *babbele* (babble)!" This was in the 1960s, when Italians were the new wave of guest workers. Despite my different color and culture, and their shared Catholic backgrounds, my exoticism and the rarity of people like me elevated my status above "the guest workers." When I met children in the neighborhood and tried to talk to them in my stilted German, they looked at me as if I were somehow disabled. After all, why would an adult not be able to speak clearly? I learned quickly that a prerequisite for survival in such situations was a sense of humor, a friendly smile, . . . and learning the local language as quickly as possible. I had to keep it simple. I envied the ease with which children spoke and the simplicity of their expressions.

In Frankfurt, I was introduced to Theodor Adorno, previously Heribert's doctoral supervisor, at whose illustrious institute he was employed for 4 years before leaving for Berkeley and then South Africa. I had previously noted how intimidated his fellow students were by the professoriate. I had learned that many were so much in awe of Professors Adorno, Horkheimer, and Habermas that they did not dare to write original pieces for fear that they could never be good enough. This was largely the fault of the luminaries because effective teaching would have liberated students if their work was considered routinely as worthy of discussion. Instead, they stood as passive, sycophantic observers of the brilliance of their teachers. Protected by my outsider status and ignorance, knowing only Adorno's work on the authoritarian personality, I had no fear of the greatness of the master. When I shook hands with him, my immediate surprise was how soft his handshake was. I had expected a firm handshake by someone of his stature. Adorno primarily perceived me as an Indian and hardly asked me about the political situation in South Africa under apartheid, which I assumed a person with his awareness might have found of interest. Instead, the conversation moved to his experience with Indians he had met at Oxford. I was surprised that Indianness as a category took central place in the otherwise very pleasant exchange. Africa was obviously off the radar.

After my meeting with Adorno, we were taken to a very special lunch by Professor von Friedeburg, subsequently the regional Minister of Education. At the end, he proposed to Heribert a renewed position to work with him at the Institute. Heribert treated the offer with respect, thanked him for it, but mentioned that unfortunately we had decided to take up an offer in North America. The relationship dramatically cooled off and we left at almost freezing level, with repeated utterances of feelingless "good wishes" and "all the best." To reject such an offer at such a venerable institution was tantamount to rejecting the fatherland! After such betrayal, Heribert did not receive any more invitations or correspondence from his former employer.

From the mid-1960s, student protest was in its heyday. Heribert took me to many teach-ins and demonstrations in Berlin and Frankfurt where we listened to the likes of Rudi Dutschke and Daniel Cohn-Bendit, among others. University campuses were cold, heavily smeared with graffiti, with battered walls and slogan-gouged windows, in sharp contrast to their South African and American counterparts. Everything spelled destruction and disaffection and I wondered what kind of society had produced such anger and nonidentification with a place of learning. Philosophers like Adorno and Habermas and well-known editors and journalists like Karl Heinz Bohrer interpreted the unfolding trajectory of student resistance of that period in different ways. Habermas, the radical democrat, viewed developments as civil disobedience—unprincipled activists considered direct action as more significant than "dominance-free discourse." The dialogue between philosophers and students, aided by considerable media exposure, was uniquely German. Students argued for street activism while Frankfurt intellectual leaders viewed theorizing also as activism. The sole focus on sociological issues broadened to include psychoanalysis, psychiatry, and social history. This established a connection between social justice and personal unhappiness under capitalism. No precedent of this nature, at this level, existed in North America. Yet the rapid decline of a positive discourse between radicalized students and professors dependent on state support and recognition was epitomized in the humiliating derision of Adorno in 1969. Students interrupted his main weekly lecture before a large audience calling upon him to engage in "self-criticism," saying, "If we leave Adorno in peace, capitalism will never cease." When Adorno turned to leave, three women students dressed in leather jackets and with flowers came up to the stage, bared their breasts, and sought to kiss him. Such undeserved mocking actions, making fun of his proclaimed sexual emancipation, aimed at a narcissistic and sensitive person, not only shamed and embarrassed him, but left him deeply devastated and wounded. I assume it contributed to his untimely death from a heart attack a few months later.

My entry to life in Berlin, then a divided city with a heavily fortified and guarded wall in the middle, was something quite different. Driving from Frankfurt to Berlin required passing through another formidable border, the Iron Curtain. Our car was checked and stood over a mirror to make sure no one was being transported beneath. One had to get through the corridor within a certain time. On one occasion, my partner, either risk prone or chronically forgetful, hadn't filled the gas tank sufficiently, and we ran out of petrol. It was a dicey situation, parking on the side of an East German autobahn, but fortunately a gas station was within walking distance, while I waited in the car.

In Berlin, Heribert introduced me to friends living in a classy commune, not far from the Goethe Institute on Knesebeckstrasse, near Savigny Platz, just off the fashionable Kurfurstendamm. The art deco apartment had beautifully decorated tall ceilings. It looked quite elegant though they were all living on a student budget. The owner had great style and furnished the apartment with beautiful pieces of art and porcelain that she was able to find at flea market sales. With discerning taste, she filled her very basic IKEA shelves with even some Meissen porcelain pieces she had managed to find. We stayed with them for the first two weeks before renting our own room in the parallel Uhlandstrasse with a bar fridge and single electric cooking plate, where my first lessons in cooking were to begin.

In the commune there were four regular residents. The vivacious female head of the household, Hanne Herkommer, also a graduate of the Frankfurt Institute, proudly admitted that she followed "Teddy's"—as Adorno was colloquially called—recommended career choice. Adorno had suggested that she would be best suited as a translator working from home for a publishing house, which would allow her to look after her then newborn daughter. The suggestion to follow this as a low-paying but respectful occupational option, which was hardly a career path, would certainly not have been the advice a male student would have received. Women's careers at the time were also heavily dependent on being available to

pick up children at noon, when the school day ended, to serve them the customary one hot meal of the day at midday. Women were constrained, not only by this
custom, but by the school hours, which began very early and ended in time for
lunch. To all intents and purposes she was a single mother estranged from her
husband who was a visiting professor in England. Her live-in lover at the time was
a much younger, long-haired student, a "super-liberated" type, averse to the pleas-
ures of frequent showers and personal grooming. The fourth communal member
was a cerebral Frankfurt sociologist, Wilke Thomssen, specializing in educational
research at the Max Planck Institute in Berlin. Because his wife had a teaching
position in Frankfurt, it was decided that he would work in Berlin during the
week and visit his family on the weekends. Heribert was the godfather of his young
daughter, then living with the mother in Frankfurt. The men in the commune defied the usual male stereotypes in division of labor. They took turns picking up the
freshly baked "broetchen" and making the coffee for breakfast. Wilke, in fact, was
a gourmet cook with enviable culinary skills. He delighted in cooking with me,
assuming I had all the know-how about Indian cooking, which I didn't. However,
having watched my mother who did Sunday lunches and special dinners, I was
able to pull off some creations they loved with little comparative basis to judge.
Nor did I dispute this.

Germans at the time were so keen to show off their English language com-
petency that any word I asked them about would ascend into high levels of subtle
distinctions between variations of possible meanings both in English and German.
They represented the height of individualism and were all politically engaged,
theoretically sophisticated, and well-informed about ongoing events in a climate
of high student activism. Frankfurt and Berlin were the main sites of student re-
bellion.

In 1965 the Auschwitz trials in Frankfurt had begun to publicize more widely
the deeds of the perpetrators of inexplicable barbarism. A new postwar generation
questioned the behavior of their parents and grandparents. Nazi collaborators in
the government, like Hans Globke, were singled out for denigration, and the whole
political establishment was delegitimized as a continuation of the past. Students
also denounced the traditional hierarchy of conservative universities: "Unter den
Talaren der Muff von 1000 Jahren" ("Under the gowns, the mold of 1,000 years").
Empty houses were being occupied as justified expropriation of capitalist wealth.
After demolition notices were served, there were student parties to smash as much
as possible of the existing structures. The country was in upheaval. A sexual re-
bellion had already taken place. Questionable slogans such as "sleep with the same
girl twice and you're part of the establishment" captured the frequently derailed
rebellious energy of the time. Marriage and monogamy were viewed as bourgeois
institutions. The fashion at the time was not to bear children because they limited one's activist capacity and intellectual work, but also because of the undesirable nature of the world into which children would be brought. Coming from a
warm country where children were overcoddled and the center of the family, one

example remains with me to this day. When our commune friends went out in the evening, the mother of the 4-year-old spoke to her child as if she were an adult. She mentioned that she would be going out and wouldn't be far from home. After she had bathed and fed her and put her in her bed, she told her that she would be locking the door and there would be no need for her to answer the door if the bell rang. What surprised me was the total acceptance of the child without showing signs of fear of being alone. This would never have happened in our community in South Africa, and it would be considered illegal in Canada to leave a child unattended at home under the age of 12.

After those initial months in Berlin and Frankfurt, we planned a proper wedding ceremony in the summer of 1968 to be held with my and Heribert's family and friends in a rented home in Stierstadt im Taunus. When preparing, my parents asked Professor Varadarajulu, who was a colleague in religious studies at the university in Durban, if he would tape-record the wedding service in Sanskrit, which we could use. He was very hesitant to do this for fear of coming under the scrutiny of the university administration for sanctifying an "immoral" marriage, as well as my being an ostracized outcast. However, he eventually agreed to record the service for us. And so we were married in the large manicured garden of the rented house by my mother using the tape-recorded Sanskrit service. Everything was improvised. The children's sand pit became the base for a flower-decked canopy, with four posts covered in summer blossoms. A beautiful Roman marble pot, unearthed on the property from an earlier excavation, contained the sacred fire. Upon the recitation of Sanskrit chants, beautiful fragrant shavings of wood were fed into the fire, to bless the couple and bring the families together on this auspicious occasion. There was a ceremonial exchange of garlands between us promising a shared exchange of everything each one had, which was not much. We agreed to the custom of taking seven steps together, promising to care for each other, grow in strength, share joys, share sorrows, care for parents and family, be together forever, and, the one we liked best, remain lifelong friends. About sixty guests watched, mingled, and were even happy with vegetarian food and nonalcoholic drinks. Indian marriage ceremonies were usually conducted by "Pundits," who were men, and were much more elaborate. Ours was a modified ceremony. It indicated the incredible flexibility and fearlessness of people like my parents who were ready to defy traditional customs and find new ways to address nontraditional situations. After news of our marriage appeared in a front-page article in South Africa's *Sunday Times,* our relatives' responses to the news of my marriage to a European were told with good humor. One aunt tried to pacify my parents by saying, "You shouldn't worry, even Indira Gandhi's son is marrying an Italian girl." Another more accepting uncle consoled them: "Don't worry, she's ahead of her time. In the future, what she is doing will be quite common." Then came the rural aunts who said, "What can you do? It is her fate . . . this is put out for her." But most classic of all was the ultimate aunt who said, "You know, at least he's not an Englishman!"

Heribert's mother and family, too, must have found it difficult as a believing Catholic family to have what must have looked like "heathen rituals." In fact, his uncle who was a Catholic priest and rector of the University of Mainz, refused to marry us according to Catholic rites, since I was a non-Catholic and Heribert had long abandoned Catholicism. So began our formally married status, after we had signed the necessary papers at the magistrate's office and I had requested to retain my maiden name, not very common at the time. To my surprise, a cherished German passport had been automatically prepared for me to sign, requiring that I surrender my South African one. Fearing that I might never be able to return to South Africa by renouncing this birthright, I declined the German passport.

Germany became our second home, which we frequently visited on numerous stopovers or conference invitations and spent research semesters at the universities of Marburg, Siegen, Freiburg, and Berlin. We always chose these opportunities to enroll our children in German schools. In Siegen the Waldorf School especially was impressive for instilling fluency in a new language. In contrast to Berlin, we lived in a renovated mill in a forest in a village with nine farmsteads. A villager told us there were just seven houses 400 years ago. The children arrived there without any German. Within a few weeks they began to connect with children in the village and were fluent when we left after 4 months.

The country never ceases to amaze me for the way in which the past has been addressed. They invested an enormous amount of thought and finances into keeping alive the conversation about their unsavory history. Every schoolchild is exposed to the reality of how anti-Semitism grew during the Nazi period. Educational programs aimed at addressing these questions while focusing on antiracism, scrupulously avoided the term *race* even as a social construct for fear of reinforcing that *race* was, in fact, real. Preferred foci were on "intercultural education" and "anti-Semitism."

Yet in my lived day-to-day experience, racial differences did, in fact, play out, however benignly and unjudgmentally. A visit to the hairdresser gave rise to the differences between Asiatic and other hair types; a visit to the pharmacist raised the question of the suitability of certain kinds of medication "for people like me." I was frequently told we Asiatic types have a peaceful temperament. Years earlier, when I was expecting our second child in Germany, I experienced the workings of a German hospital. After it was determined by virtue of the kind of medical insurance we had and because I had the deferred status of being "Frau Professor Dr.," the Herr Professor who headed my medical team came over to me in my well-screened-off area to let me know, "You will hear many loud cries, but you shouldn't worry about it, these are only Italians." When our child was born, her cries were described as "temperamentful," so characteristic of swarthy-skinned folk like me.

All this said, Germany is the only country in the world where a monument of shame was built in the center of the capital. Extensive public consultation took place for years about the form the monument should take, followed by further discussions as to whether it should be dedicated to all groups who were victims of the Holocaust or just to European Jews. Continuing education keeps the awareness alive. Each visit to Berlin after this period reminded me of the many attempts to memorialize the past. There are at least five first-rate Jewish museums in Berlin in addition to several other Nazi remembrances. At Bebelplatz, previously known as the Opernplatz, is a flaming monument to remind one of the May 1933 public book-burning of un-German books. They were those published by Jews, liberals, left-leaning writers, pacifists, and foreigners. Students from 20 German universities participated in the planning of this project, with the assistance of a librarian who helped in developing a list of blacklisted books. A consequence of the blacklisting was the exodus from Germany of authors like Brecht, Freud, and Thomas Mann among thousands of others. Often cited is the sentence from the 19th-century German Jewish poet, Heinrich Heine, who wrote in his 1821 play, *Almansor*: "Dort wo man Buecher verbrennt, verbrennt man am Ende auch Menschen" (Where they burn books, they will also be burning people). Another ongoing commemoration was initiated in various German cities by the sculptor Gunter Demnig. He placed brass plaques either on streets, marking where a synagogue once stood, or on sidewalks and on buildings, engraving on these plaques the names, birthdates, when and where residents were taken, and the death camps where they were killed. These memorialization tablets are called *Stolpersteine*, or stumbling stones. Each plaque reminds, disturbs, and moves. These developments seek to make whole again, a country shattered from an inconceivable past.

Then there is the other part of Berlin that I enjoyed after my 4-hour-long language class: a walk on the Kurfürstendam, its glitziness notwithstanding, to meet Heribert, spend time browsing in the excellent bookstores or walk to the KaDeWe, the most fabulous store with every possible delicacy from the world on its upper food floor. Though we could ill afford the prices, we occasionally splurged and spoilt ourselves. And then just sitting to people-watch while we sipped Berliner Weisse on the boulevard. Berlin had wonderful niches that attracted different publics, like the Literature Café on Ulandstrasse in a classic older building and a cultivated old garden. One was always certain to meet interesting people to converse with.

In Frankfurt, in December 2019, we visited again the extensively renovated History Museum and Roemer, the center of the city where kings were once crowned in the nearby Dom, or cathedral. Surrounded by glittering Christmas markets, the traditional offerings of gluhwein, apfelpfannkuchen, and kartoffelpuffer were now extended to Turkish, Thai, and Indian specialties with curry in every possible offering. The culinary scene is perhaps one of the few areas one notices that the population of Germany, which now comprises a hefty percentage of people with a migration background, has changed since I first arrived in the late 1960s. Yet the new citizens do not feature in the national image of Germany, other than as incidental inclusions.

A greatly worrying trend is the rise of neo-Nazi and extreme right-wing groups, particularly in Dresden and Sachsen, where relatively few foreigners ever settled. Anna Sauerbrey (2017) highlights a marked difference in the way in which extremism is handled in the United States compared to Germany. Americans openly marching through the streets of Charlottesville with swastika-decorated flags would not have been allowed in Germany. It is illegal to display Nazi symbols in Germany, out of respect to victims of the Holocaust. Similarly, incitement to hatred, *volksverhetzung,* which denigrates groups on the basis of religion or ethnicity and promotes hatred and violence, is punishable with up to 5 years in prison. Furthermore, extremist political parties that threaten the political order can be banned by Germany's highest court, the constitutional court. In the United States the argument used against the German approach is based on the constitutional right of freedom of expression. These two countries have very different political cultures. Much hinges on "faith in a democratic public to police itself."

Many Germans are keen to educate their children in a second and third language. Every German child is now proud of the ability to say a few words in English or French. Whenever parents can afford to, children are sent to an English-speaking country to gain fluency. Others hire English-speaking au pairs. When I taught a course at the Free University of Berlin in 1999, one of the suggestions given was that at least half of the course readings should be in English. As my husband was preparing himself to teach in his native German, he was told he could teach the course in English, as most German students were quite comfortable with English. Even more recently, I was asked by a German sociologist why I took the trouble to learn German. She said, "There's not that much literature in the social sciences that's worth the investment of time to learn German." I was taken aback, impressed with her nonchauvinistic approach to her language. I replied that I loved the depth of the language in literature, and it had opened new vistas for me. Besides, I had enjoyed the contacts with people that speaking to someone in their own language opened up for me. It reminded me of Mandela, during his incarceration on Robben Island, learning Afrikaans, the language of the then dominant group, so that he could reach them at an emotional level.

With this in mind, both our daughters spent time learning second and third languages. Kanya, our older daughter had spent many summers in the French perfume region of Grasse practicing her school French. On one of these visits, she befriended a neighbouring family who asked if we would consider an exchange with their son, which we did. He was Edouard Phillipe who years later became the French Prime Minister. She spent several months with his family in Paris, while he spent the time with us in Vancouver improving his English. Subsequently she studied German in Berlin and upon returning to Vancouver began taking Hindi classes.

In the early 1990s our younger daughter immediately after high school decided to pursue a career in ballet, which began in Germany. Her stay there provided us with many opportunities to visit Stuttgart at first, and later Dresden, where she performed as a soloist at the Semperoper. Two impressions remain with me. She mentioned how the director and the staff communicated with all the dancers as if they at any time should be fluent in French, English, Italian, and German in receiving instruction. And they did exactly that! Everyone learned fast in context. At the time, there was a widespread concern about the fate of German culture and the number of foreign artists now performing. One day, driving through Stuttgart, I saw a large banner hanging from the Stuttgart theater, which read "44 nations work together here to keep German culture!" It left an indelible impression on me, to see a counter-position to what might otherwise be a narrow nationalist version of identity.

CHAPTER 9

Experiences in Egypt
My Entry to the Middle East

At the end of 1971, after a few years in Canada, Heribert was granted an administrative leave and a 1-year sabbatical. As with many new immigrants, I was still on 1-year teaching contracts at various Vancouver schools, not dissimilar to the fate of new immigrants who always have to enter the workforce at a level lower than their previous experience. With the option of a long leave, we decided to explore a developing country and settled on applying for the American University in historically rich but financially impoverished Egypt, rather than in glamorous Beirut, with the hope of traveling and learning about the wider Middle East. A dean from the American University in Cairo (AUC) spent a full day looking us over in our Vancouver home, probing above all whether we were subversive radicals. We must have satisfied him because a few weeks later a 2-year contract (1972–1974) from the institution arrived. The offer stipulated a good salary for teaching two sociology courses per semester, covered airfare for our family of three, "home leave" with generous baggage allowance, and a rent-free furnished three bedroom apartment in the heart of Cairo. So we chose to free ourselves from being property owners in preference for this new life experience. We decided to sell a newly purchased but unoccupied house in West Vancouver, on which we had just put a down payment. We rapidly discovered there were additional expenses related to first-time homeowners that we would have had a hard time covering anyway—selling was a release from unanticipated financial encumbrances.

Our first night in a university-owned apartment in the Zamalek district of Cairo turned a little traumatizing when masses of huge cockroaches scampered across the floor as soon as the lights were turned off. When we complained to the university authorities, they were most responsive in relocating us quickly. The alternative Cairo apartment they found for us was a stone's throw from the Nile, on the third floor in central Dokki. Our apartment, on a quiet tree-lined side street some two hundred meters away from the once-fashionable Corniche el Nil near the Sheraton Hotel and almost opposite the German Embassy, we later learned had just become available because the previous CIA occupants had been expelled from the country. It also explained to us why the entrance was still guarded day and night by three friendly uniformed policemen—really illiterate peasants with guns keeping a watch out, they said, for the "philistines" (Palestinians).

We had envisaged an interesting life in the chaotic city but did not realize what it meant on the ground. Egypt, under President Sadat at the time, was still in the Soviet orbit. Nevertheless, Russians were unpopular because they were opposed to *bakshish,* the lubricating bribe that smoothed all services and interactions with officials. Ordinary necessities of daily life, from cheese to sugar to toilet paper, were in short and erratic supply, and required long queuing, which our *Bawab,* the cook in a long *galabaya,* was keen to join because he could also earn a bit extra from the shopping. The cook's profession was to serve us three meals a day. It involved endless decision making on my part about what he should prepare. Not accustomed to such regulated three meals, to which our digestive systems weren't responding well, we had to shorten his offerings to prepare just one meal, dinner. Clearly, I did not fit the image of "the madame" whose life revolved around eating and entertaining. I dressed simply and was younger than most madames he was accustomed to. Working on my doctorate and having a 2-year-old to care for preoccupied me. We had also brought my youngest sister, Subithra, who we thought would benefit from continuing her studies at AUC, especially in light of the political unrest at her South African university. My parents were relieved to have her in a safe environment away from the possibility of disrupted studies and possible arrest for involvement in the protests on campus. Though we had little, Heribert, the ever-thoughtful person that he is, arranged to enroll her at the American University in Cairo and was very supportive of her living with us for the 2 years while she was a student. In so doing, he was simply carrying on the family tradition of sharing whatever we had.

Entering Egypt with a South African passport was always a challenge. There was a time when we returned from one of our visits to Beirut that Heribert with his German passport was allowed to reenter Cairo, but I had to remain until the Head of Customs and Immigration arrived to give special permission for a South African passport holder to enter. The Egyptian rationale for excluding South Africans, while being politically admirable in ostracizing South Africa for its apartheid policies, was ironically keeping me as a Black South African from entering. Meanwhile, Heribert mobilized the university authorities to intervene, and I'm sure with a little "greasing of palms" by the university administration, my entry was hastened. Similarly, when my sister Devi arrived to visit us for a month in Cairo, she was kept for three days at the airport, due to heavy rains, until approval could be arranged. Finally, again with the assistance of our university contacts, we were able to obtain permission for her visit.

The apartment block had some very interesting colleagues also attached to AUC. There was John Waterbury, who later became the president of the American University of Beirut; Martin Hinds, who was an Arabic language scholar from Cambridge, and his wife Pamela; David and Nahid Waines, he a Middle East historian and she a Lebanese psychologist. We often hung out with them at the Gezira Club in Zamalek, which was included in our contract, where our children could swim and play in the lush green gardens in the heart of the city.

AUC had presented us each with a handbook of rudimentary Arabic phrases and words to facilitate our everyday functioning, which was most helpful. We were provided with contact information for health- and travel-related needs, shopping places and markets, and an American interpretation of local cultural habits. Since phenotypically I could be taken to be Egyptian, people constantly spoke to me in Arabic. I had to learn quickly. Smiling was not enough. Coming from a multilingual South African childhood, I had unknowingly learned the art of mimicry, an essential part of learning to play with languages. I soon learned the appropriate phrases and gestures and to say less rather than more to cover for my restricted grasp of the language in use. To begin with, this language was unlike any other I had been in contact with. The words for "yes" (*aywah*) and "no" (*la*) had no bearing on any of my prior languages. I now realize how totally unprepared I was upon arrival. Quickly, the importance of learning phrases and the way people communicated in context became one of my best ways of gaining the limited mastery of daily conversation. Phrases to make people amused helped positive daily contact. I learned, too, how to retain authority in a situation by saying very little. On one occasion, a Canadian woman, Mary Prestas, who had helped to babysit our first child in Vancouver for the first 18 months of her life while I was teaching and doing postgraduate studies, came to visit us in Cairo. She had been a registered nurse who told a neighbor that she was looking out to help someone who could benefit from her support. Under normal circumstances we could not have afforded to have 5 days of babysitting. But with this wonderful offer at a very reasonable rate, we had benefited greatly from her expert and loving care. When we decided to go to Cairo, we were delighted she could visit us. One day as she and I sat in a taxi going to the pyramids, to avoid taxi drivers taking advantage of us as foreigners, I whispered to her at the back of the cab not to say anything as they would know we were foreigners. After a minute, this silvery-blonde, blue-eyed woman and I burst into laughter thinking how ludicrous my comment was since there was no way she could be local. I had forgotten entirely about her appearance compared to mine.

Everywhere we went, one was expected to hand out a *bakshish* or tip. When Heribert didn't, he was asked if he was Russian. The taxis were in a dismal state, and on one occasion as I was travelling to the local market, the bottom of the taxi fell out and my feet were on the road beneath, as were the driver's! The classic response with outstretched hands was *ma'alesh* (nevermind). I have never seen such a positive-spirited people in the face of every adversity. American visitors were amazed at the incredible kindness and generosity of local people toward each other in the face of poverty and overcrowded conditions.

A little different, however, was our experience when on one of our drives to the pyramids, our taxi pushed over a woman who fell to the side of the dusty road. When he refused to stop to see if she was hurt, as we pleaded for him to stop, the driver responded that "she was only a peasant!" We felt powerless in the middle of the countryside. We made a vain attempt to take his cab number and name to report the incident, but never heard back.

Life in Cairo teemed with surprises daily. When I looked out of the apartment window on certain days, I saw that everyone deposited their garbage in mounds on the sidewalks. Within a few hours, poor people looked through them and took what they could rescue. Later in the day, shepherds brought their goats who cleaned up whatever was left and the street was totally cleared of garbage. This offered some lessons in recycling, at first worrisome to newcomers like us anticipating the worst of garbage piled up.

When I needed medical supplies and handed in the prescription to the pharmacist, he—yes, it was invariably a "he"—said in Arabic, "Sorry, we don't have it today, but it will come." When I enquired, "When?" the answer with a smile was "*Mumkin bokara, mumkin badi bokara! Mumkin badi badi bokara*" (maybe tomorrow, maybe the day after tomorrow, or maybe the day after that). My husband's Germanic expectations of punctual delivery took some reeducating.

During our time there, the Six-Day War broke out between Egypt and Israel. Egyptians felt very proud of what they considered a victory over the enemy. As Canadians, and myself still a South African passport holder with a Canadian Landed Immigrant visa, our situation was vulnerable. We sat on our packed suitcases, ready to be evacuated at any time, though it never came to that. In a trivial vein, sometime afterward when things had settled down and life was normalizing, I tried to buy a tablecloth at the market, and wanted a white one, not a yellowish cream one, so I asked the seller if he had a white one. His reply, in exasperation, I will never forget, "Madame, in these days of war, what is the difference between a white tablecloth and a yellow one?"

Freedom of speech or an independent media existed mainly in the nostalgic memories of foreigners. The only Egyptian English-language newspaper covered mostly government announcements and events. When election results were announced, the ruling party had achieved a 99% approval. When the 30 students in the sociology class were asked who of them had voted on the previous day in the much-celebrated election, only one hand went up. The American University of Cairo was an enclave of privilege for the upper class in the middle of the city surrounded by high walls overgrown with greenery. Women students came in their acceptable street clothes and changed on campus into the most fashionable Western outfits, often acquired in Beirut, London, or the United States. Before and after classes they relaxed in rattan chairs on the well-watered green lawns sipping espressos or Turkish coffee in small cups. *Galabaya*-clad waiters were constantly in attendance refilling from beautiful brass containers, with the accompanying gestures of obsequiousness, customary when serving privileged ladies. Since Egyptians were extremely generous and hospitable to foreigners, we were invited to fashionable, antique-furnished, high-ceilinged apartments with ostentatious displays of polished silver and fine china. The tables were always laden with large platters of well-prepared food, so typical of the prevailing culture of hospitality. Nothing gave greater pleasure to the hosts than if we accepted their frequent offers of food for us to enjoy. Impressive, too, was the way in which people shifted from English to Arabic and French with great ease. The multilingualism of this class of people revealed Egypt's history of Mediterranean and African migration over centuries, which became integrated into all aspects of daily life. In the Middle East, multiple origins of infinite variety seemed coherent and unconflicted in defining individual identities. We rarely saw evidence of the Islamic fundamentalism that was to follow. Yet we sensed tensions between Muslims and Copts, who kept to themselves. During Ramadan we were awakened by the sounds of the muezzin calling on worshippers to rise at the break of dawn and at sunset. Moving indeed was the sight of the poor workers who had fasted all day, breaking their fasts with the simplest of food—pita bread, some green onions, a few fava beans or cheese. By contrast, the wealthier homes had tables laden with wonderful foods to break their fasts before the day of fasting ahead. Dinner consisted of different meats, grains, and salads, to be followed by the sweetest of sweets.

Teaching critical social science in an authoritarian system, whether apartheid South Africa or Egypt, is not impossible but requires circumspection for the challenges lurking. Teaching in a dictatorship, an instructor can generally assume the presence of informants. The danger is that they report incorrectly according to their comprehension of what was said. An instructor in an authoritarian system faces the danger of imprisonment or expulsion. For criticism to be disguised by offering a range of perspectives, an opportunity for debate is created. Formulated without negative or positive value judgements, students usually arrive at their own opinions.

Overall, our Cairo experience introduced me to a North African–Mediterranean cosmopolitanism, especially insofar as people of color effortlessly used different languages and cultures seemingly coexisted harmoniously. Color or "race" played less of a role in hierarchy than did income levels and poverty. My colonial education, with its emphasis on well-spoken English language as the only hallmark of the educated, underwent a major transformation. I had never before seen people who looked like me in positions of power, using non-English–dominated codes of communication with such facility. In the Middle East multiple origins seemed coherent and unconflicted in defining a person's identity. At the same time, sub-Saharan Africans continued to be stigmatized, going back to the Arab role in the slave trade.

Another problematic feature of segments of Arab society was misogyny. Foreign women traveling alone on buses and trains felt unsafe and frequently reported being molested. Totally neglected from our social conversations in cosmopolitan settings at the time was the underbelly of regressive social customs to which women were subjected. Nawal El Saadawi's psychological research on women and sexuality remained banned for decades and only published in Beirut. In 1972, when it was published in Egypt under the title *Women and Sex,* she was dismissed from her position as director of Public Health. She attacked genital mutilation as violating and demeaning ritual practices on women's bodies, which she herself had endured at the age of 6. At the time El Saadawi estimated that 90% of all Egyptian girls had suffered this. Even more disturbing was the role of mothers in supporting the procedure. Only in 2008 were clitorectomies declared illegal in Egypt. When

El Saadawi was interviewed much later in 2015 as to whether things had changed since then, her reply was instructive of the lurking caveats:

> No, it has stayed the same. You can't change such a deep-rooted habit by passing a law. You need education. The law was passed to satisfy the West. They wanted to cover that disgrace, not to eradicate the practice itself. You have to change the minds of the mothers and fathers and even of the girls themselves, who have been brainwashed to accept it. (Cooke, 2015)

Our stay in Egypt provided an entry to several visits to neighboring countries. We made frequent visits to Beirut, which was a beautiful city then. Our friend Theo Hanf had a deep interest in the region, and we had many discussions on the complexity of the intergroup relations in the area. Several conferences followed and I especially gained much from participating in a conference in Byblos on the outskirts of Beirut.

Beyond Lebanon, one memorable trip was in the company of the Canadian diplomat George Cowley, Counsellor in the Canadian Embassy in Cairo, and his journalist wife Debbie Cowley. We visited Syria, taking a cab from Beirut to Damascus in mid-winter. The cab driver, whose wife was expecting a child, made a point of stopping in a mountainous area to collect some snow in a bottle to take to her. When asked why, he said they would then have a child who had a complexion as white as snow. Arriving in Damascus we found a culturally and historically rich and a fascinating city. Noticeable was its absence of beggars, unlike Cairo. Whether this was due to Russian influence or an edict by an authoritarian government remained unclear.

Since there were no flights between Egypt and Israel, we visited Israel by traveling via Cyprus, but ensuring that no Israeli stamp was entered in our passports, which would have resulted in a rejection of re-entry to Egypt. This visit marked the beginning of valued contacts, which grew and lasted over decades, with Israeli and Palestinian social scientists and historians. Among these colleagues are Daphna Golan, Mahdi Abdul Hadi, Rema Hammami, Andre Mazawi, Fouad Moughrabi, Benny Neuberger, Sami Smooha, Bernie Susser, and Mottie Tamarkin. During my term as president of the International Sociological Association's Research Committee on Race, Minority and Ethnic Relations, together with Nira Yuval-Davis we organized two conferences in 2000 in Israel at Tel Aviv and Al Quds Universities. It was an honor to work with Sari Nusseibeh, then president of Al Quds, and to be exposed to the complexity of reasoning as to the desirability for different parties of the one- or two-state options at the time.

I never returned to Egypt after our 2-year stint in Cairo ended in 1974 and our second child, Maya, was due. We had searched in vain for a hospital in Cairo in which we felt confident in case of complications, and opted instead for a hospital nearer the family home in Germany. Our exposure to the Middle East showed its lasting impact more than 30 years later when I embarked with my husband on a book addressing the Israeli–Palestinian conflict: *Seeking Mandela* (2005). We asked: What can be learned from South Africa's negotiated revolution for peace-making in the Middle East? Is a South African–type common society feasible, inevitable, or preferable to a two-state solution in Israel/Palestine? We probed the widely held assumption that had Mandela been the Palestinian leader, the conflict would have long been resolved, and questioned whether such personalized magic could succeed in the absence of other South African preconditions for a negotiated settlement. The Nobel laureate J. M. Coetzee endorsed the book with the support-ive comment: "Stepping firmly into a notorious minefield of ethnic/religious pas-sions, Adam and Moodley argue convincingly that hoping for some savior figure to bring the warring parties together is futile. For the uncompromising quality of their political analysis, and for the tough realism of the advice they offer, they are to be applauded." However, the applause from our friends on both the Jewish and Palestinian sides was hardly forthcoming. Each side saw us as not being sufficient-ly critical of the other. In our view, uncritical solidarity elevates fallible policies into the realm of the sacred. If students remember nothing else from this book on an intractable Middle East conflict, it has been worthwhile.

CHAPTER 10

An Immigrant in Canada

We arrived by air in Montreal in the late summer of 1968 and made our way to the wharf to pick up our little Fiat with our main possession, a heavy typewriter, in its trunk. We must have looked a young, naive, and innocent pair, as a Quebecois immigration official looked at us and said: "Why are you going to Vancouver? It's a place where old colonial generals go to retire. You don't belong there, stay here! It's much better for people like you." Against his advice, we drove across the country for 5 days, on endless highways and through miles of corn and wheat fields, staying in one motel worse than the last.

When we arrived in Vancouver, it was a gray, rainy day. All I remember was a huge billboard advertising English bone-china teacups. We found ourselves on the east side of Hastings Street near Pidgeon Park where a number of inebriated figures gathered under a tree to take shelter and smoke. We figured this was the downtown area of the city. Heribert went in search of a barber shop, and then we wanted something to eat. There was a barbershop sign and he went into it, to try to make himself look respectable. Each of us was hiding from the other our true feelings of "what have we come to?" But we overtly stayed positive and caught glimpses of the North Shore Mountains to elevate our moods. Then we entered a place with four stars that advertised seafood. When we got in, our appetites disappeared, neither of us wanted to eat anything. We stared at the bowl of clams, as much as the clams seemed to stare at us, and we left without a bite to eat! Still, we weren't admitting to each other our shock at where we had landed after being in Berlin and Frankfurt for the last half year. We drove up to our first meeting at Simon Fraser University (SFU) on Burnaby Mountain. Sometime later, we realized that we had first arrived on the east side of Vancouver in Skid Row. Our instincts about our disinclination to eat were not totally off!

I remember the grayness of the concrete building at Simon Fraser University, the day we arrived. Meant to be an architectural feat of Arthur Erickson, it was touted as imaging the Acropolis, designed to bring students and teachers together into a center they could not avoid passing through. The bleakness that received us upon our arrival, and not encountering a single familiar face, did not help. Unknown to us, Tom Bottomore, a noted scholar who had hired Heribert, had left with thwarted aspirations to create a Canadian version of the London School of Economics. Derided as a mere Marxiologist as opposed to a Marxist activist, he had moved on. Heribert was to meet some of his colleagues for the first time and suggested I join him. Our first coffee together was in the cafeteria, in the company of other very vociferous colleagues, clearly engaged in bringing the ivory tower down. They avoided the bourgeois niceties of recognizing we had just arrived in Canada for the first time, not a word to lead us into the ongoing conversation. Cussing and complaining about the administration and the need to expose its exploitative practices was our introduction. They seemed to assume that we were privy to all the evils of the institution. We, of course, had far more mundane things on our minds. Where is the department and office located? Where can we find a place to live? Which building is the library on campus? So we gazed from one speaker to the next, in the glazed manner of the newcomer, I at least only half grasping all that was being said. It was like being shown the way with signposts we did not comprehend. One thing that remains with me to this day was the lack of the of personal warmth that African society exudes, to which we had both become accustomed.

Many impressions remain with me. We contacted one colleague, Gerry Sperling, who kindly offered us to spend the first few nights with him. At 5 in the morning his four dogs tore into the house and jumped onto our bed; at 6:30 he took a shower and sang loudly while he bathed; the house hadn't been cleaned for some time ,and he was clearly comfortable in its laissez-faire atmosphere. His wife, Linda, was away so he was distractedly fending for himself, clearly unfamiliar with his kitchen.

Finally, we were told about the availability of the house of an economist about to be vacated since he planned to be away over his sabbatical. He and his partner, apparently an expert on imperialism, obviously left in a hurry having many things to attend to before their departure. Abandoned unwashed dishes and a greasy cast iron frying pan were left in the sink. Everything smelled of mold. Dust billowed from the well-worn sofas when we sat in them. But the rent was right. The house was clearly "radical chic," brimming with eastside character, grungy, located beside what had been two abandoned grain silos, a romantic sight overlooking railway tracks and the harbor through a large glass window. We pulled out the colorful East African pieces of fabric I had brought and covered the old sofas. We must have looked like the epitome of committed counterculture types. Our unwashed Fiat with a German license plate, parked on the street, had the word *Kraut* scrawled on the dirty windshield.

It was the 1st year of our marriage. Coming from South Africa, where I lived in my family home, I had little expertise in housecleaning. Due to my own incompetence, the more I cleaned, the less it changed the way things looked. I had never done a large load of laundry before by hand. No washing machine was available and I had yet to learn about public laundromats. Here I was handwashing Heribert's shirts and our other laundry. When it came to drying, I suddenly had visual memories of driving by the townships in South Africa, where people who did not have enough space on the clotheslines or wire fences, placed the wet items on the overgrown grass, which held them off the ground. Having no clothesline, I hung out the laundry around the edge of the bathtub, and then when there was no more room, I put items on the overgrown grass. Seeing me in the yard, the neighbor came to the fence to say hello, but suddenly realizing that he had left his set of dentures in the house, he hurriedly excused himself and came back with the mug holding his teeth, putting them in right in front of me.

I spent some time bemoaning my situation, looking at the condition of my previously nice nails, feeling sorry for myself that this was my fate in a first world country, as a newlywed. When we married, we were both equal as working individuals. How easily I had slid into this role of doing the laundry, ironing shirts, preparing food. Mainly, this was of my own doing. Well-intentioned Heribert tried to iron but lingered too long on one spot, resulting in several burnt patches. Even my poor cooking skills trumped the Hawaiian toast and the beautifully plated open-faced sandwiches with German sliced meats and pickles we ate all too frequently when he tried to make dinner. In self-defense, I voluntarily took on more and more to ease the situation. After all, to be fair, Heribert had his tenure track position first, in a new country, in a new language, and I was unemployed. That winter things got even worse. It was the coldest in years, the plumbing froze, the toilets were unusable, and we were 90th in line for the plumber to come to us. One look at me when the plumber finally arrived led him to say, "I only take on first-generation customers." I had not expected this in Canada. I remembered yearning for South Africa, apartheid and all. People may not have had large houses and fancy appliances, but warmth, kindness, and friendship flowed freely. People helped each other in times of need. Financially, Africans may have had little by comparison, but in human relations, in sharing, in helping each other, they excelled. Every immigrant must go through these thoughts, revisiting what was, glorifying, romanticizing in exaggerated colors the contrasts of what is and what was.

In the midst of all of this, my sister Devi, who was studying in Kansas, came to visit, and her face conveyed a repressed message of "what on earth have you come to?" Though she mouthed encouraging words like how beautiful the first snow was in Vancouver, I could see the discomfort. Nonverbal messages have a way of getting through louder than words, and sisters are taskmasters at receiving, sending, and interpreting such messages.

Over time, another colleague we got to know was Ian Whitaker, an English anthropologist, who kindly invited us to his home. He was a single dad, who had a home with a very English feel about it. There were collections of cake and candy tins with photographs of the royal family, a little kitschy I thought to myself. In the living room were the foreboding portraits, painted in deep Rembrandt-like colors, of rather severe-looking men. Casually, he dropped hints that these were his ancestors, interspersing the conversation with attributes and temperaments of each. Years later it emerged that Ian's sister was an antique dealer; his English colleagues alluded to the possibility that these portraits were chosen from her collections obtained from auctions and recycled as legitimate ancestors. He remained a superior "classy" colleague compared to us, simple immigrants, who lacked the gloss of fine ancestry and the appropriate accent he so masterfully wielded. He played the role of the English anthropologist very coolly, and on one occasion came to visit us in his four-wheel-drive jeep, wearing a T-shirt with the saying "Insanity is inherited. You get it from your kids!" All this said and done, I realized that my colonial past notwithstanding, or perhaps because of it, shared universes of literature read, and sense of humor strangely enough made for a certain warmth in the contact with the likes of Whitaker. And all the more so with the very hospitable English historian, Martin Kitchen, whom we warmed to. His sophisticated sense of humor, his incredible knowledge not only of the German language but his unbelievable ability to imitate German dialects, continue to amuse us to this day. With him we could effortlessly glide from one language to the next, and with his knowledge of historical detail, there was never a dull moment.

My entry into the job market as a new immigrant was not easy. Although I had taught courses on sociological theory in South Africa, my entry point in the new country was as a teaching assistant. Then came an opening at Vancouver Community College as instructor. Though poorly paid, it was interesting because of the students who enrolled. They were all mature students who worked and took part-time instruction, which was less expensive and would lead them to university admission later. In my course on sociological theory, one student of Indian origin was very modest and reserved, and when I drew him out in informal discussions during breaks, he mentioned having come from the Punjab via a short spell in the United Kingdom and found work in a lumbermill. This was Ujjal Dosanjh, who became a respected politician, then premier of the province of British Columbia and a member of the Liberal Prime Minister's federal cabinet. In his memoir he mentions, among other things, how my wearing of Indian clothes on occasion when I came to teach made him feel comfortable. This reminded me of the neglected role of being taught by people one experiences as sharing similar universes. Another student was the son of a very volatile lawyer, Phil Rankin, who became a prominent immigration lawyer. And another student was a discrete, well-spoken young woman, Maria Tippett, who raised a polite question about whether there were any women theorists that would be part of the course. I remember thinking on my feet and mentioning I would like to include Rosa Luxemburg and Hannah Arendt. This marked, for me, a learning moment of how unquestioning I had been about the "classical theorists" in terms of gender. This student subsequently went on to become a well-known author of some fifteen books, won several writers' awards after completing her doctoral work in history at University College London and later at Cambridge. She and her astute Cambridge historian husband, Peter Clarke, are now valued friends on Pender Island, our British Columbian retreat.

My next career move was to seek a position at university level. A friend suggested that since it might be difficult for me to work in the Sociology Department at Simon Fraser University, where my husband was employed, and impossible for me to gain a faculty position at the University of British Columbia (UBC), where I had completed my doctoral studies and they never hired their own students, that I try related fields. Before I left South Africa, I had obtained a graduate teaching diploma and for a short while taught high school English. So I was introduced to the Simon Fraser faculty where a course on "Cultural Differences in Education" was being taught and a vacancy for a 1-year appointment existed to replace a faculty member on leave. This opened new possibilities for me. I quickly grasped the dangers of limited education about "cultural differences," catchy though the title seemed, and its promises of instant knowledge about how to include "differences" in developing a well-meaning approach toward the achievement of social justice in education. Two comments from student interactions during the breaks left me with an indelible impression. One student mentioned he had only time to learn 10 things he should and shouldn't do when dealing with a Sikh population, or any other ethnic group. He was in this course for a quick cost-benefit. Another student mentioned why Black students have difficulty swimming: "Its simple," she said, "their bones are heavier." I realized the importance of letting students air their own opinions, and the danger of misinformation, "a little knowledge," and the lure of ill-grounded simplistic "differences." Above all, what appeared uppermost was the need for a deeper, critical education.

Part of my work at Simon Fraser entailed coordinating a program, Spring Insitute for Teacher Education, in their distance education program in Kamloops, a small town in the Okanagan region, about an hour's flight away from Vancouver, once a week for 2 days. My time away from home on these days was not without emotional costs to our younger daughter, who, I learned later, hung on to my scarf during my absence to smell the perfume I'd used. There was a budget to invite guest speakers to the Kamloops SFU Center. Among several invited speakers was the most eminent scholar in the field, James Banks of the University of Washington in Seattle. He generously agreed to travel to Kamloops to speak to the wider educational community in this area. This opened up a valuable contribution to their understanding of how multicultural education addressed the needs of the diverse population, initially of the United States, but broadened to have global significance. From this beginning emanated, for me, a long collaboration on many publications and conferences. Other valued inclusions in this series of lectures, was the British psychologist Chris Bagley, whose work on cognitive styles in learning focused on the United Kingdom, and Stan Shapson, on bilingual education in Canada.

With these beginnings, I was able to fill an unexpected opening at UBC when a Cuban faculty member abruptly abandoned the position she held without advance notice. I had applied to UBC previously and though I never received a response, my details had obviously been on file and they contacted me. I was indeed available, but packing to leave to take on a 1-year invitation with my husband at Yale University's Southern Africa Research Program. I interviewed for the position anyway, and they agreed to hold the appointment until I returned.

On my second visit to Ivy League Yale, we again traveled by car, but this time with our two young daughters and a tent in the trunk. Crossing the Canadian border somewhere in middle America, the suspicious U.S. customs official asked about our destination: "Yale? Is this a recognized college?" While at Yale, we rented a comfortable home in nearby Woodbridge. We worked and socialized with the somewhat autocratic founder of the program, the eminent historian Leonard Thomson; the savvy Stan Greenberg, who later became the pollster of Bill Clinton and also advised the ANC at election times; but above all Hermann Giliomee, with whom Heribert coauthored a book on Afrikaner nationalism, *Ethnic Power Mobilized: Can South Africa Change* (1979).

During this stay in New Haven, I learned more about the deep divides not only between "town and gown" but between White and Black inhabitants of the city. On campus, I had heard of the valuable research being conducted by a Black American psychologist on the deep psychological effects of continued denigration on Black youth. She and I established a good rapport and friendship grew. I was honored and excited about an invitation to dinner at her home one weekend. When Heribert and I arrived, we faced a very formal dinner situation, uncustomary in a university setting. Guests wore fashionable black-and-white attire, just one grade below a black-tie affair. Furthermore, Heribert was the only non-Black guest. While they expressed great interest in me, my South African life and observations about the United States, not one person engaged with Heribert in any way during the entire evening. Afterward, I was impressed with his graceful acceptance of the situation when he commented to me: "Well, that was an informative situation for me. Now we know what it feels like to be the only invisible Black in the room!" At that point I was glad to be married to a social scientist!

Upon our return to Vancouver in 1979, the sizeable UBC Education Faculty of over 100, mainly male, teaching faculty included no visible minorities other than the newly appointed dean, Vince D'Oyley, who was of Jamaican origin. He was most supportive and later mentored me, suggesting that if I intended to play a role in public life as he had, it was important to join one of the community organizations to "locate" myself. I understood what he was getting at. It brought home to me what multiculturalism meant in reality. Identifying myself as a member of an ethnic organization would strengthen access to state funds to assist in furthering minority recognition. Were there tinges of my South African past in this?

My first teaching assignment was one I consider to be the most meaningful of all. I was asked to teach a section of my Sociology of Education course in the Native Indian Teacher Education Program (NITEP) on the North Vancouver Indian reserve. Without total comprehension of the situation, I learned that several other senior colleagues had refused to teach a course separately to any group, on principle. Rather selfishly, and understanding the rationale for the program, I welcomed the opportunity to broaden my knowledge of issues facing First Nations people in my adopted country. Once I got to know these students personally, the course took the form of making these concepts relevant to their own situation. At the same time, the focus sought to extend their horizons internationally to understand how different types of minorities coped with factors impeding their social mobility. My own life as a student in apartheid South Africa, where the White instructor in 1st-year Sociology left us silent in tutorials because he spoke only at abstract conceptual levels with little relevance to our lives, sensitized me to seek alternative ways to foster dialogue and critique. That cohort of about 12 students taught me more than I did them. This program aimed at creating a smaller, more focused offering to increase the attractiveness of a career in teaching to First Nations students. Its size, focus, and intimacy overcame the alienating effects of a large anonymous campus, which had in the past led to a high dropout rate. So successful was this program that more First Nations faculty were hired. A responsive vice president, Dan Birch, in collaboration with Verna Kirkness, a First Nations program leader, gave the initiative further visibility and support. An architecturally striking building was erected called the First Nations House of Learning, providing a welcoming and supportive base for First Nations students at the university. When a position became available to teach in this expanding program, I naively applied, only to learn through innuendo that the position was intended only for those with First Nations origins. I received neither an acknowledgment of my application nor a letter of rejection. I read between the lines and realized it was a faux pas to have applied at all. I should have known. It reminded me of the "gentleman's agreement" we Indians in South Africa were supposed to honor by not making offers on houses advertised for sale in White areas.

The second alternative program at which I taught, called LISTEN (Low Income Studies in Teacher Education), was aimed at teacher education for working in low-income areas of the city. A cohort of about 25 students was taken through all the teacher education courses and taught with an emphasis on the special needs of children from low-income families and communities. Their teaching practicums were located in schools in the Downtown Eastside, where we first arrived in Vancouver. Reflecting on the program as a whole, the sociology of education component offered exposure to social justice issues, the role of class, gender, and racism in education. I do recall one field trip and the drive with the students from the UBC campus in one of the highest income areas in the city, through middle-income areas, and finally to the downtown inner-city enclaves. The students observed the changing spatial and environmental aspects as we drove: size of living spaces; the quality of school playgrounds, some with grass playing fields as opposed to concrete and gravel areas in others; the parks and access to beaches; proximity to highways polluted by heavy traffic emissions. Apart from that, there were few specific pedagogies that applied to each area of the program. Some of the research about the class difference in parenting styles bordered close to generalizations and stereotypes. Retreats with the students and faculty, meant for group bonding, served the purpose of gaining personal background information about students and their Achilles heels, which might have been better left undetected. Did such retreats, I sometimes questioned, enable greater control? They didn't always work to students' advantages. I will never forget one student's informal comment to me about how she felt fortunate that her teachers did not know about her parents' alcoholism, so that she was treated just like everyone else and did so well at school. She felt free of being labeled as a student at risk and no one held lower expectations of her.

After the program had operated for about six years, schools were reluctant to offer practicum opportunities to our students from a program labeled "Lower Income." Some schools rejected it as a negative approach. After much consideration in the faculty, it was decided to redefine and relabel the program as Multicultural Teacher Education Program (MTEP). Since I had coordinated the last year of the LISTEN program, I reconceptualized the direction of the new program focus. Each subject area attempted to incorporate material that was reflective of the diverse composition of the students in their schools and classrooms, ensuring that it was thematically related and well integrated. I was especially proud of my Anthropology of Education course in which students collaborated on studying different neighborhoods as an ethnographic study. Such a hands-on study I intended would let them discover the history of shifts in the ethnic populations in an area over time. The actual living conditions of their students influenced by different economic factors, lifestyle preferences, and consumption priorities would provide a dynamic view of immigrant integration as evolving and being reshaped in the new context.

We used the Museum of Anthropology, a teaching museum, as a great resource. Here students could understand the relationship between environment and culture. They could access material cultural artifacts and learn not only about their function within First Nations communities, but also how different cultures shared similarities in their use of materials. We did have one problem when three First Nations students decided they would not participate because it was disrespectful of the spirits of their ancestors. I said it would be helpful if they would talk to us about it and explain this further. After we had a discussion and students conversed with each other, the dissenting students reassessed their positions and joined us. They were satisfied with the motives of the other students to learn more about the history and backgrounds of First Nations people.

The Sociology of Education course exposed them to theories of social justice, Canadian immigration history, welfare state policies, race and racism and their impact on women, and indigenous and immigrant minorities. A section of the course opened up how second language learning can be incorporated through an additive approach as opposed to erasing first languages. This discussion about second and third languages revealed the notable absence of any First Nations languages in the offerings. It gave rise to how this came about through residential schools, with assimilation policies that punished First Nations students for using their languages, and gradually led to their demise.

Another focus we explored in this program was the lived worlds of the communities surrounding us. We visited places of worship and what they told us about religious diversity in operation. This led to a visit to a Sikh Gurdwara, a Buddhist temple, a Hindu temple, an Ismaili Jamat Khanna, a Jewish synagogue, a Unitarian church, and a Catholic church. Students learned about each institution, the spaces, the aesthetics, the highly placed value on books and knowledge, how children move about freely during the services in some and not in others, the meals some institutions provide to the public through regular lunch services to anyone visiting, and a general introduction to their philosophies. Comparative religious knowledge is not taught at all in Canadian schools for fear of sectarian conflicts, which actually are prevented rather than incited by those insights.

To my dismay, I was shocked to see that I had failed to instruct the students about appropriate dress and manners for different settings; I assumed they knew. Some came in very short shorts and exposed tops. Some were chewing gum. When we went to the Buddhist temple, two of the monks present had taken vows of silence and would not speak. One of the woman students thought it quite funny and tried to taunt the monk into responding by joking with him. An elaborate debriefing afterward ensured that they learned about appropriate, respectful behavior. I should have known better. Many North American students are raised in just one communicative style for their friends, their parents, and formal settings. Switching code to communicate appropriately in formal and informal settings has never been part of their socialization. As potential job applicants, this would be a valuable skill, not out of deference but simply as appropriate for each occasion.

All in all, the size of the student cohort and its collaborating faculty who had chosen to work in this alternative program had the optimal structural features for a coordinated caring framework. The broader insights into culture, class, and racism served to educate through discovery rather than indoctrinate.

FORAYS INTO INTROSPECTIVE CONSCIENTICIZATION

Teaching graduate courses as a visible minority professor in the Faculty of Education on multiculturalism and antiracism education to a multiethnic, multicultural, and multiracial class, my aim was to be as inclusive of every student as possible. I had observed from past practices how easily the course opened up the space for minority students to feel comfortable sharing their experiences in what seemed to be a safe and accepting environment. Suddenly some previously quiet students found they had a theme on which they could enter the conversation. At the same time, the situation took the form of silencing White minority students into being perpetrators, the converse of their usual experience. The former seemed a positive thing and I could see my own visible difference as an encouraging factor with the unspoken promise of a safe space. I was reminded about my own education at University level where, in the presence of imperious White professors, we did not dare to voice a comment in class. As a teacher, did I not have the responsibility to create an inclusive environment for all my students? My usual opening of the seminar was to ask each person to tell a little about themselves and what brought them to the class. There were always surprises about the range of experiences students contributed. Many had lived in other countries, learned another language, often a non-Western language, and knew what it was like to be an outsider in culturally homogeneous countries. How could one mobilize those lessons to be shared? For one of the initial assignments, I requested that each student write a 3–5-page paper after they had interviewed their parents, grandparents, or caregivers about their lived experience upon arrival in Canada. What languages had they spoken prior to arrival? How easily or with what difficulty did they make their entry into the labor market. What networks helped them with entry into the new country? What was the role of immigrant organizations or religious communities in facilitating entry? If they brought children with them, what were their experiences with the teachers and schools? What was it like to learn a new language and access medical help?

The background to these questions lay in the ethnic demographics of Vancouver. Canada admits annually about 0.9% of its total population as immigrants (300,000), twice the number of the United States and Australia. About 85% of these newcomers eventually settle in the three major cities: Toronto, Montreal, and Vancouver. In the Vancouver metro area, about half of the residents were not born in the country. According to the 2016 census, the "total visible minority population" that originates mainly from China, India, the Philippines, and the rest of the world, is slightly higher than those with European origins.

Encouraging students to reveal their different autobiographies to the rest of the class led to a discovery of similarities and differences of European and non-European experiences as newcomers. It also led to exploration of how immigrant children are placed in an inverse role with their parents because of their better grasp of the new language. Limited intergenerational communication is often even worse between minority youth and their first-generation immigrant parents experiencing language difficulties, new cultural styles, and struggles to gain acceptance and status in the country of immigration. In this respect, an exercise requiring information about parental pathways elevated their histories as worthy of recording. A student wrote: "I have enjoyed this assignment and feel it is a valuable exercise for every person. It has caused me to ask my parents questions that I might not otherwise have ever thought to ask. Nor did they ever volunteer information about their early lives."

ATTEMPTS AT INSTITUTIONAL TRANSFORMATION

The state-initiated policy of multiculturalism had a ripple effect on universities that were becoming noticeably different in student composition. In 1988 I was approached by the office of the president of UBC, David Strangway, to serve in an advisory capacity to seek ways to be a more inclusive campus. He had a very sound network at the international level, but how could linkages with local communities be fostered? How do we project ourselves to the communities we represent? All of these were deemed necessary if we were to extend equality of opportunity, as well as a sense of ownership of an otherwise Anglophile institution. Behind these noble intentions may have also been the hope that caring for the ethnic diaspora could loosen some financial taps from well-endowed locals as well as from the homeland. The university's connections with Asian countries at the international level resulted in student exchanges. A number of donors from Asian communities funded centers and buildings at UBC such as the Chan Centre for the Arts, Liu

Centre for Asian Studies, and the Ritsumeikan Centre. Subsequent concerns the university faced were the running costs of these new additions, not covered by the donors.

My role in the office of the president aimed at identifying systemic barriers in university practices, raising faculty awareness of potential for inclusiveness in curriculum development, and increasing opportunities for interface between community and researchers on campus to their mutual advantage. Why were most honorary doctorates given to White males? Have we scouted more broadly to see what we find worthy of honoring?

One approach to forging links with the community that was undertaken was to set up a series of well-publicized public forums to connect our research with questions of relevance to the public. One forum addressed the concerns of minority parents about the use of mother tongue languages at home. Did this impede children's opportunities to grasp English language fluency? What were the findings of major research studies in the area? Another session addressed intergroup relations in a multiethnic state; and a third, the role of media in race relations. The aim of these sessions was to extend the connections between the public and university research on these topics. From these initiatives many contacts grew with community groups, school boards, and the city of Vancouver in developing its race relations policies.

What warrants mention is the opposition of many senior faculty members with established research records, who saw the president's initiatives on multiculturalism as having little bearing on their own research outputs. They preferred to continue working the way they always had without questioning the changing nature and needs of society. Especially visible minority faculty saw this as highlighting their ethnic origins and thus detracting from the integrity and quality of their research, which they considered as transcending identity issues.

At the federal level, the Employment Equity Policy was being implemented in Canada. A federal contractor's program required that all institutions receiving in excess of $200,000 from federal sources would be required to show evidence of goals to make their workforce more diversified. The four target groups were: First Nations, women, visible minorities, and persons with disabilities. It would require the collection of workforce information, an analysis of the current composition, and the establishment of short- and long-term goals toward this end. The university administration was most supportive in the development of a Human Rights Policy, and a Sexual Harassment Policy, among others. Most notable of all was the facilitation of campuswide participation in the development of these policies to ensure identification and commitment to their implementation.

COMPARATIVE ENCOUNTERS

Following my period at the president's office, I held the David Lam Chair, which provided an opportunity for more comparative research on race, ethnicity, and culture. Since the early 1990s when apartheid collapsed in South Africa and the cold war ended with the dissolution of the Soviet Union, a global conference season seemed to have started, and I was invited to present papers on many panels. Six such occasions still remain firmly etched in my mind during these 2 decades.

Breyten Breytenbach, the illustrious Afrikaans poet, eccentric artist, and 7-year political prisoner in Pretoria, had invited me to a conference on Language, held on Gorée Island off the coast of Senegal, in 1998 (Moodley, 1999; 2000). Here George Soros's Open Society Foundation had established a Pan-African Learning Centre. We had challenging discussions with Neville Alexander, who had been imprisoned with Mandela on Robben Island, among others. The visit to the House of Slaves from where millions of Africans were shipped to America was incredibly moving. A third of the human cargo died on the way. In March 2000 I presented a paper on "Ethnic Strife and Democracy" (Moodley, 2001) at a conference jointly sponsored by the Library of Congress and the Law Faculty of NYU. Three Supreme Court Justices—Ruth Bader Ginsburg, Sandra Day O'Connor, and William Rehnquist—participated in a memorable exchange with a cast of international academic specialists.

Jim Banks and Cherry McGee-Banks, perceptive and wise colleagues from Seattle, had organized a weeklong seminar in 2001 on race and ethnicity with a group of U.S. and international academics at the Rockefeller Foundation Bellagio Center in Italy. I still remember details of valuable discussions with Jim, Cherry, and Amy Guttman, who has published significant work on democratic education and multiculturalism.

In November 2009 Theo Hanf from the University of Freiburg, an expert on Lebanon as well as South Africa, had put together a conference in Beirut on "The Political Function of Education in Deeply Divided Countries." It was helpful to test my paper "Canada as a Divided Society or as a Model for Multiethnic Cohesion?" on academics from a country plagued by the opposite of cohesion.

A conference invitation to Montreal in 1997 with the leading Canadian philosopher Charles Taylor first intimidated me, especially when Pierre Trudeau, former prime minister and the founder of Canadian multiculturalism, was in the front row of the audience. Only later did I relax, when Trudeau congratulated me privately despite my critical remarks. I'm not sure if it was just out of politeness or sincerely meant, but generous it was!

In November 1998 during a sabbatical in Freiburg, my husband and I were invited for a joint talk by the publisher Schlettwein in nearby Basel in Switzerland. The firm specializes in the history of Namibia. At the dinner afterward I was seated beside a gentleman by the name of Dieter Gerhardt. He was the former commander of the South African navy base in Simonstown, a spy for the Russians for 20 years, and sentenced to life imprisonment for treason in 1984. His release in 1991 was a condition Yeltsin set for restoring Russian diplomatic and trade relations with South Africa. My pleasant dinner conversation focused on how many Western spies he was worth in the exchange, how his marriage to his second wife, Ruth, came about, and how much he appreciated Mandela's praise for his antiapartheid spying and not for the money he was paid by his Kremlin handler. Gerhardt has been described as "the biggest spy since Philby," who "did the greatest damage to Israel" and United Kingdom military projects (Ancer, 2019, p. 44). Gerhardt was granted amnesty by the TRC and was temporarily employed by the new ANC government to train their spies. The spying couple disappeared from public view and apparently do not grant any interviews, so I was fortunate to have had this unexpected opportunity. When the hostess commented to me that Gerhardt came frequently to walk their dog, I joked about whether she was sure the dog did not have a chip implanted. For a fleeting moment, she looked at me, as if I might be on to something.

At UBC, I was involved in various small workshops, but one major event stands out in my memory. In July 2001, as the David Lam Chair with a small budget, I cosponsored an international conference on comparative multiculturalism, attended by the then Federal Minister, Hedy Fry, the South African High Commissioner to the United States, Franklin Sonn, academics from France (Sophie Body-Gendrot), Israel (Mottie Tamarkin), South Africa (Milton Shain, Michael Savage), and graduate students. After the 1-day public part in Vancouver we moved by boat with 25 participants to a more intimate 3-day workshop at Clam Bay Farm on Pender Island. During one of the heated discussions, a distinguished UBC professor, the late Barry Morrison, became offended by what he interpreted as a racist accusation by the High Commissioner. Raising his index finger, he said, "Don't you accuse me of racism!" Franklin Sonn replied, "You remind me of P. W. Botha!" (the former South African president with this habit), and invited the Canadian political scientist to step outside to settle the dispute physically. As the chair of the session, I had to use all my calming skills to avoid a diplomatic incident.

After several decades of teaching in Canada and spending a year at Yale and frequent visits to our daughter in Palo Alto, California, the differences between the United States and Canada in policy and reality became much clearer to me. In Canada, the traditional notion of "immigrant" had shifted on three counts: firstly, from essentially European to visibly different newcomers; secondly, from largely poorer immigrants with rural origins to a broader spectrum including skilled and financially well-endowed immigrants with urban origins; and thirdly, from a one-time migration to a new country of adoption to well-traveled global immigrants who are world citizens living among regions as diverse as Hong Kong, the Punjab, Beirut, Italy, and Vancouver. For many, Canada offered excellent economic opportunities, except for personal recognition and status. Hence many immigrants led a compartmentalized existence. Their working lives were spent here, while recognition and status were but an airline flight away. Initially frequent visits to the country of origin gradually became more and more infrequent until the comforts of a sanitized Canadian state assumed primacy in the hierarchy of needs. The traditional cyclical model from arrival to assimilation, therefore, has become obsolete in Canada, mainly due to these changes and the official policy of multiculturalism. In contrast, the majority of American citizens still do not own a passport and therefore travel only internally. Nor does the United States have an official policy of multiculturalism, as Canada proudly displays.

In South Africa, with a policy of separate development where ethnic identity was imposed, the rationale of "cultural differences" and the term *multiculturalism* had negative connotations.

In Canada, the policy of multiculturalism had been criticized by the right for its potential divisiveness and its threat to national unity and from the left for assuming that power and class differences can be overcome by the celebration of diversity and mutual tolerance. Yet, as I was to learn, Canada, as the most post-modernist society, distinguishes itself by its very pluralism, variety, and diversity. The essence of Canadian identity lies in its absence or at least its vagueness. This country is not an emotional "community of dreams" from which nationalism draws its sentimental force. Canada is a polity of heckling regions at best and a collection of shopping malls and sports stadiums at its worst. There is little hero-ic national history to draw upon, no royal house, presidency, or revolution that provides a founding unifying myth. Canada is a state of convenience in a rational mold. Unlike the United States with its public school system specially geared to generate loyalty and make patriotic little Americans out of immigrant children, Canadian education historically stressed imperial loyalty to the Crown, not to the nation. In Quebec, the survival of the French language is emphasized. The two solitudes, Anglophone and Francophone, prevented a strong Canadian identity. Where the Americans invented a special flag and rituals around the national an-them, even the singing of the national anthem "O Canada" has been only discrete-ly used. Canada does constitute a nation in the political sense, in that a person either holds Canadian citizenship or not.

In a cultural sense, however, one may be Canadian in varying degrees. That freedom of self-definition of ethnic identity should not be undervalued, compared with the assimilative pressure of American and European nationalisms. Though a nostalgic conservativism considers Canada to have been cursed with a weak na-tional identity, it is the lack of a clear homogeneous self-image or single identity that amounts to a blessing for minorities. There is the flexibility to have a say in the evolution of national identity rather than being absorbed or being assimilated into a society that initially is not theirs.

How then do we understand the ethnic enclaves of cities like Vancouver and Seattle? What role do they have to play? The segregated ethnic enclave is often contrasted with the assimilation/integration model. A cultural ghetto, one reads, can be either voluntary, as in the case of religious communities, or it can be forced through discrimination and closure of access. A group's enclosure is often fostered and forced by the surrounding hostility. The greater the opposition—economic, political, social, or religious—which is perceived by the ethnic group, the greater the appeal to its sense of distinctiveness and the greater its solidarity. The relative absence of ethnic cohesion therefore would indicate little discrimination. In the absence of hostility toward newcomers there is less of a need to cultivate ethnic bonds, though there may be affective needs that bring people together. In this respect, much overlooked are the specific needs of communities based on their traditional aesthetic and culinary tastes. When trading enterprises satisfy these needs, linkages are established that reaffirm connections with countries and regions of origin. Nor are the benefits of such traditions confined to the group alone. Increasingly, the broader society incorporates these tastes into changing palates and lifestyles. At the same time, ethnic community formation is celebrated as a welcome political resource. "Gatekeepers" and "power brokers" of the establishment perpetuate ghettoization of newcomers, while ethnic entrepreneurs present themselves as mediators and interpreters of community needs. Immigrants in a new environment can fall back on the advice and assistance of their peers. Contacts with familiar people understanding common home languages offer a comfort zone.

But what of the tendency to hire only in-group members in the pursuit of this noble goal of integration? What of the hostility aroused in nongroup members who feel excluded by the specification of "_____ only" job advertisements? Is this acceptable in terms of the broader canvas of an integrated society? If we always treat minorities as victims only, there is an in-built condescension that locks them into a passive mode as people who need to be understood, assisted, and helped. Is there is a reciprocal role that needs to be implemented? That we *all* need to model the kind of inclusive society we wish to be part of? If ethnic exclusiveness is not desirable elsewhere, can it be defended within the enclave? Does the agency, or capacity to create the type of society we value, not lie in all groups?

Finally, with the admirable zeal to eliminate the pernicious effects of systemic racism and create an equitable society, Canada has institutionalized a laudable equity policy. To ensure adequate monitoring of the process, the 1996 census for the first time officially gathered racial identity statistics. Even as a necessary benchmark for measuring the progress of equity programs, racial census figures could lend themselves to abuse. Could there be a call for overrepresented Asian minorities at universities to be reduced, as was the case for Jewish applicants at U.S. universities? Could popular stereotypes ascribe certain criminal behavior to specific minorities? Might racial crime statistics then legitimize racist police behavior through profiling all minority members as automatic suspects?

I often asked my students to critically reflect on the question: Do we need this racialization of Canadian society? A shortsighted, polarizing color consciousness may exacerbate the very stigmatization that intended antiracism aims to destigmatize. Can the ideal of color blindness ever be achieved through state sponsored color consciousness despite its transformative purpose? The need for antiracism strategies notwithstanding, it is also time to reassert the ideal of a common humanity that finally lays to rest "the figment of the pigment."

CHAPTER 11

Political Literacy as Strategy to Combat Bigotry

Various questions are on my mind in considering the most academic chapter of this journey: How does one synthesize the many presentations made worldwide on race, culture, identity, and nationalism? How can this reflection avoid repeating what has been conveyed in this book explicitly and, even more, implicitly? How can I define precisely my understanding of *political literacy*? How can I best illustrate the application of this literacy for the teacher in the classroom? Do such reflections apply universally or must they be specific to South Africa, the United States, Europe, and Canada? How can I place the concept in the context of the vast literature on citizenship education? On the assumption of more or less universal validity with some local variations, I begin with a segment of the vast literature with which I am familiar, followed by comparisons between countries and interpretations of relevant historical events.

REFLECTING ON SELECTED ASPECTS OF THE LITERATURE

International comparative research has shown that civic education impacts on bigotry and nationalistic sentiment in different ways. However, a consensus has emerged that the right type of political literacy combats bigotry effectively. Michael Hjerm (2001), who surveyed eight European countries plus Australia and Canada, concludes: "Levels of nationalist sentiment as well as of xenophobia decrease with increasing levels of education in all the countries examined, despite substantial differences between the educational systems in the countries" (p. 37).

South African political education has focused mainly on voter education around electoral procedures and processes. It has regurgitated the history of the Liberation Movement and celebrated struggle heroes. It has neglected critical analysis and moral education in enabling citizens to arrive at mature and informed judgments in ethical predicaments. How education for active, participatory citizenship can transform a historical reality of inequality into a new better life for liberated people has defied solutions thus far. Increasing evidence suggests that new nonracial injustices are even harder to combat than the more overt, morally discredited, previous racial system. Therefore, antiracist education in South

Africa has to be broadened to include other kinds of racism as well as possibilities of despotism against fellow citizens. Civic education for a dominant group needs to focus on protecting democratic safeguards and constitutionalism, rather than merely making space for neglected cultures in the curriculum. A vibrant and self-confident South African Black culture with an established rich linguistic base survived internal colonialism because of its critical mass. It was also not territorially displaced and subject to assimilationist pressures, as were immigrants and indigenous minorities in the Americas.

Most of the European and American literature on educating citizens in a multicultural society concerns itself exclusively with the problem of integrating minorities and immigrants into the mainstream. Particularly in the U.S. context, powerless minorities of color battle prejudice from the outside and struggle to maintain dignity and self-esteem within marginalized communities. Antiracist citizenship education aims at "cultural, economic and political equity" (Banks, 1997, p. 123) and making "full Americans" out of variously excluded residents. In Europe, sensitizing the majority to accepting difference, eschewing xenophobia, and embracing multiculturalism, poses a particularly onerous task. All Western European countries that had embraced multiculturalism (Germany, France, United Kingdom) have officially abandoned it. In any case, educating for multiculturalism rarely transcended the approach of intercultural education, namely understanding "the other," although in reality they are growing more multicultural. In fact European societies never really implemented multiculturalism the way in which Canada did, to allow them to speak of abandoning it. The answer to this lies in the very fundamental ways in which these societies differ from one another with regard to immigration and citizenship.

Citizenship equalizes inhabitants of a state by bestowing on them identical rights and obligations, regardless of their other differences. At the same time, citizenship for locals only, or increasing the hurdles for acquiring citizenship, excludes "foreigners" from access to such entitlements, including voting rights, Living and working in wealthy states, and participating in welfare benefits by joining the social contract of citizens, represents a much sought after privilege by persons from impoverished areas. Economic globalization and growing transnational migrancy have made immigration regulations one of the most contested political issues, particularly in the United States as well as European nation-states.

Based on the pioneering work of the British philosopher Bernard Crick (2000) and subsequently that of Anna Douglas (2012), *political literacy* refers to the skills of inquiry needed to understand the ways in which power operates in democratic and autocratic social contexts. The aim is to acquire basic knowledge through a critical reading of the way institutions function and an understanding of how democracy works in practice at local, national, and global levels. At the same time, political literacy is more than political knowledge and more than citizenship education. Within the framework of human dignity, equality, and social justice, political literacy also focuses on the process of deconstructing the causes of social conflict, the way in which diversity works, and the nature of dissent in society. The underlying goal of acquiring habits of staying critically informed on current events is to engage in transformative action by shaping democracy through the use of well-formulated, reasoned arguments. In most of the scholarly educational litera-ture, political literacy is viewed as a tool and precondition for young people to be-come active and engaged citizens. Political awareness flows from knowledge about public issues and motivates political participation. Henry Milner (2002) defines *civic literacy* as "knowledge required for effective political choice" (p. 59). Con-trary to the view that center parties increasingly resemble each other, justifying passivity rather than participation is the case of the United States. Recent political polarization and racialization has clarified the choices to reverse anti-democratic trends through voting.

Any issue in the public domain can be considered political. Feminists have long argued that even the personal is political and that the distinction between public and private affairs is illusionary. Therefore, the skill to read all issues and events politically constitutes the highest form of political literacy.

Comparative research indicates that civic education is most effective in the late high school years and in early adulthood. Comparison between Europe and the United States also reveals a higher political literacy in countries with a high level of quality media exposure (Europe) and lower in societies with what Milner (2002) calls private "television dependency" (p. 55). The quality of most U.S. and South African media, with their focus on parochial local issues combined with overreporting of crime, disasters, celebrities, and sport, compared with the deeper exposure to international issues in public television and media in the rest of Af-rica, India and other Asian countries, China, Europe, Canada, and Australia, also accounts for surprising differences in voter participation and civic knowledge lev-els. However, the use of new technologies—especially social networking interfaces like Facebook and Twitter—by young voters has the potential to overcome polit-ical apathy and mobilize large youth sectors, as U.S. presidential campaigns have demonstrated. The youth uprisings in the Arab world in societies without freedom of speech and independent media in 2010 and 2011 reconfirmed the power of in-formal communication and political discourse under repressive conditions.

Above all, political literacy not only informs about contested ideas, but en-ables a person to distinguish and make sense of competing values. Teaching polit-ical literacy merely as lawmaking, or constitutional prescriptions of how conflicts between government agencies are settled, or how scarce goods are distributed, or what constitutes good and bad governance, misses the moral and ethical issues that always underlie political debates. Such a focus on political institutions is likely to stifle political interest among students. Students are motivated when they are invited to solve political problems rather than being lectured on how a political system functions. Exposing young learners to moral controversies encourages autonomous, critical thinking. If such disputes are derived from current affairs and country-specific debates, they will stimulate active participation rather than reduce learners to passive recipients.

INTERPRETING COMPARISONS

A salient challenge for educators, then, is how these concepts can be translated into the classroom. What would be some of the moral predicaments in which students could become engaged? U.S. educators have mentioned examples in light of recent U.S. history. Is torture (Guantanamo) illegitimate under any circumstances or justified to prevent imminent terrorist attacks? In other words, could human rights violations be tolerated if lives could be saved? How much surveillance and invasion of privacy can be allowed? Who decides? In a current similar quandary: How much can normal freedom of movement, consumption, and work opportunities be restricted in the COVID-19 pandemic? Should all politicians be forced to resign if they intentionally lied to their constituents, and how can this be enforced? In light of frequent mass shootings, how much gun control should be established and should carrying of all firearms be outlawed? How can whistleblowers—workers who report rampant corruption in their employer's company—be protected? Or should they be ostracized for betraying colleagues? Does the international community have a responsibility to protect citizens of tyrannical states? Or does such intervention constitute illegitimate imperialism? Does a wealthy country like the United States have a moral obligation to admit refugees and asylum-seekers? Can it be justified to restrict poor migrants and send them back to their countries of origin? Should prejudices and extremist views of other groups be tolerated in accordance with freedom of speech values? Or should they be prohibited and criminalized as hate speech?

A useful lesson about the pitfalls and merits of political education can be gleaned from antiracism education. In the spirit of the literature, a more detailed examination of the noble intentions and shortcomings of antiracism teaching highlights the essential necessity of political literacy for teachers and curriculum designers. In the quest for social justice, attempts to counteract racism often unravel the hidden privilege of dominant groups, expose their complicity, and reinforce the dichotomy of the privileged and the oppressed in color-coded terms. Developing sensitivity and empathy for "the other" constitutes a strong component of such moral exercises. What is frequently neglected in such approaches is the political literacy that emanates from a deeper sociological understanding of racism, its functions, and its ever-changing forms. Racism is neither eradicated by preaching tolerance nor reduced by providing information that contradicts the stereotypes of "the other." Unless the predisposing conditions for denigration are addressed, the racist mind finds rationalizations for inferiorizing ever-changing targets. The behavior or appearance of the minority hardly influences the authoritarian character conditioned to prejudge, regardless of the behavior of the "other." Victims are always interchangeable. Just as psychoanalytic therapy aims at making conscious the unconscious, transforming id into ego, in Freudian terms, so the most lasting cure is to make the prejudiced individual understand why they cherish such deep resentments. As all people are prejudiced to varying degrees, this political education in the most genuine sense should be geared to everyone, not just individuals singled out for special consciousness-raising.

Political literacy, to some extent, immunizes against racist temptations. Political literacy differs from political education, which is usually considered central to the participation of citizens in government. Instead, the aim is to nurture the ability to read critically and deconstruct issues, events, and debates. It is a way of making sense of how inequality works, to understand institutional racism, comprehend how racial binaries become entrenched as well as to challenge them. Specific counteracting policies flow from such understanding, which is a precondition for successful practice.

Policies, procedures, consequences, and accountability for racist incidents need to be in place in all schools. So, too, should compulsory education in the skills to deal with a multiethnic clientele for teachers, police personnel, social workers, or hospital staff. With few exceptions, these do not prevail, despite supposed commitments to cross-cultural communication. Deterrence and communication skills, as necessary as they are, are no substitute for political literacy. It is this wider context of understanding racist behavior that is missing in most present attempts to fight an obvious evil. Instead of demonizing racism or espousing the moral superiority of the "unprejudiced," the predisposition to adopt a racist mentality has to be understood. Psychologists point to the need arising within unfulfilled individuals who are unable to establish a secure identity except by debasing others. New social conditions of individual powerlessness through automation, digitilization, and economic globalization, together with the increasing and unbridgeable wealth gap, deprive ordinary people of security and self-confidence so crucial in warding off the impulse to stigmatize others. With the decline of self-realization in a political economy where more and more people are declared superfluous, scapegoating and other artificial forms of self-realization increase.

Racism may manifest itself in individual psychology, but it also needs to be understood in relation to the social structure at large, in which character development is always embedded. In this deeper sense, successful antiracism is predicated upon societal transformation. An apolitical consumerism that prioritizes the private realm while denigrating the public sphere, however, cannot grasp the political significance of racism, let alone envisage the alternative that would eliminate the need for racial stigmatization. In short, the best job educators can do to combat racism is to ensure a global political literacy.

Such a global political literacy would be based on a sound education to provide a *historical* understanding of the nature of prejudice, discrimination, and racism. This historical knowledge would draw upon a *comparative* and *international* perspective, cosmopolitan in nature. The underlying questions would be: How do local specifics differ from discrimination elsewhere? Why do particular manifestations of inequality and exclusion develop the way they do? What role did the state, public compliance, and specific group interests play in allowing unique characteristics to unfold? Critical analytical skills constitute the motivating force to decode mythologies and demystify popular ideologies. Students are encouraged to question conventional wisdom and to develop interrogative skills in distinguishing, for instance, apartheid from fascism, old from new forms of racism, and racial, cultural, and gender-based essentialisms. Racism and xenophobia as explanatory concepts themselves become the focus of critical inquiry.

TYPES AND EXPRESSIONS OF RACISM

What this means can be summarized best by clarifying seven different manifestations of racism:

- *Legal racism* was epitomized in apartheid South Africa and the Jim Crow laws of the U.S. South, which have now been abolished. As in the case of slavery previously, public opinion and effective forms of resistance such as the civil rights movement, strikes, and economic boycotts turned against such obvious systems of inequality.
- *Scientific racism*, which was biologically rationalized, once justified colonial rule with its assertions of the superior intellectual and genetic qualities of European conquerors and its converse of inferior innate qualities of those it subjugated. It has also gone out of fashion and has become discredited.
- *Social racism* is experienced subliminally through a cultural hierarchy of arrogance and may be even more debilitating in its effects than legalized collective discrimination. It has frequently replaced the previous cruder forms of discrimination and exclusion. Social racism often justifies the avoidance of social interaction with other groups on the basis of different "tastes," preferences, and comfort levels in contact with others.
- *Cultural racism* has become a modernized form of "race talk." Utilizing the more acceptable terms *culture* and *ethnicity* for *race*, difference could be reconciled with the goal of equality without disturbing the power hierarchy. Yet through their implicit essentialized content, it served the same purpose that *race* did previously. What constitutes valuable and worthwhile knowledge neglects non-European sources. Students learn to question the assumption of universal applicability of Western values and are introduced to an understanding of Eurocentrism without necessarily embracing cultural relativism. Clitorectomy, for instance, remains a crime even if whole cultures in East Africa practice it.
- *Economic racism* survives as the most significant indicator of an unaddressed past. Unequal educational and opportunity structures, and barriers in hiring practices, serve to reinforce unequal life chances. Ethnic groups are locked into positions without chances of mobility.
- *Religious racism* of the Hindu caste system likewise stigmatizes and degrades groups, placing them firmly in an unequal division of labor. Social contact between castes is shunned at all levels. Students learn that

racism is not only a Black/White phenomenon, but it occurs wherever segments are discriminated against on the basis of ancestry or inherited group membership into which they are born and from which they cannot escape.

- *Internalized Racism.* Psychological implications of denigration and exclusion based on racism focus on how denigrated groups often internalize the dominant view of themselves. Being disempowered and stigmatized from above predisposes them to ostracize others below them or to identify with their own oppressors.

The insights gained from these broader understandings of discrimination, the similarities and differences from one context to the next, the relationships between class-, race-, and gender-based inequality, and the human costs involved all serve to educate rather than indoctrinate. They provide the intellectual scaffolding to deal with the tension between the ideal of color blindness and color consciousness to recognize just how race and racialization works. Students exposed to this kind of broad historical and comparative reasoning are thereby enabled to acquire the necessary skills to critically evaluate solutions and policies that are locally appropriate. These could range from what kind of affirmative action can best address historical disadvantage to what kind of personal involvement active citizens should have in a democratic culture.

Students in all societies need an understanding of ethnicity, nationalism, ethnocentrism, patriotism, and cosmopolitanism. I follow Anthony Smith's (1986) widely accepted use of ethnicity as "designating a historical community of cultural similarities with a shared sense of solidarity and belonging, memories or symbols or myth of descent" (p. 22). When such distinct people aim at either greater political autonomy or their own state they form a nation. *Nationalism* can be described as "politicized ethnicity."

Analysts of nationalism frequently refer to its "Janus face." The good side of nationalism consists of communal solidarity, the sense of belonging, affirmed identity, and caring and security among like-minded people with the same cultural heritage. Yet these laudable features are often overshadowed by negative attitudes of parochialism, ethnocentrism, discrimination, and racism, not to speak of aggressive expansionism in nationalistic mobilization against perceived adversaries. Too many lives have been sacrificed on the altar of nationalist wars for the glory of an imagined community.

Colonial expansion was fueled by nationalism. Nationalism aided colonialism by providing the emotional motivation to serve as cannon fodder for the colonial army. Generations of young men willingly and enthusiastically risked their lives so that the nation could live, expand, or be reborn. A particularly aggressive brand of nationalism thrives on historical grievances that it promises to redress through unity. In its quest for redress, nationalism aims at an all-class alliance. Rich and poor, educated and uneducated, men and women, merge in the fantasy of advancement in one strong whole. Being part of a triumphant nation makes for the all-class appeal of nationalist mobilization against alleged threats. Both settlers and natives have embraced nationalism.

In the great European 19th- and 20th-century wars, ancestry is elevated to the criterion of belonging. Where ancestry is not visible, religion, language, or accent serve as markers of boundaries for the in-group. The history of exclusion, anti-Semitism, and the memory of the Nazi genocide served as the main cohesive bond for diverse Jewish groups. Those features define ethnic citizenship, in contrast to the citizenship of civic rights for all legal residents in a given territory, regardless of religion or origin. States with only ethnic citizenship have also been called *ethnocracies*.

Ethnocentrism is the "glorification of one's own group." It rests on positive conceptions about the in-group, in contrast to mostly negative stereotypes about out-groups. Most enlightened people consider themselves free of stereotypes. Yet stereotypes serve as initial signposts in a complex world, ideally to be revised through counterexperiences. Everybody begins with these prejudgments or prejudices because nobody can investigate each new encounter free of preconceptions. Outsiders are judged from one's own culturally superior standpoints. However, even identical appearance and conforming behavior of the out-group does not preclude animosity. Minor differences can be exaggerated to justify separateness, as the Freudian concept of "narcissism of small difference" asserts.

Equal civic rights for citizens with different origins, some argue, lacks the emotional glue of appeals to common descent. Constitutional patriotism, the pride in a genuinely inclusive democracy, represents an ideal that few states have managed to generate. Much more common is the official or unofficial recognition of ethnicity. An *ethnocracy* usually privileges in-group members. Ethnic citizenship thrives on the dichotomy between indigenous and nonindigenous, between those who belong to the nation and those who are strangers, newcomers, or migrants from somewhere else. With the narrative of returning home after 2,000 years of absence, Zionism has reversed the indigenous–alien distinction: Jews have instantly become natives and Palestinians alien foreigners in the eyes of the new settlers.

Generally speaking, and as Germany past and present proves, even if "strangers" are "naturalized" or "nationalized" in the sense that they acquire all the habits and attributes of natives and identify with the "homeland," they remain nonnatives from the vantage point of ethnic nationalism. For example, most German Jews had totally assimilated to German virtues and vices, even fought in World War I with the same fervor. Yet abandoning traditional identity did not save them from Nazi paranoia. Second- and third-generation Turkish migrants, born and educated in Germany without any Turkish cultural traits, are still not "real Germans" in private perceptions, despite their German passport. Likewise, fifth-generation White South Africans or third-generation Indians, regardless of their political identification, are still not considered "Africans" in the social and customary sense. With globalization and increased migration, the rifts between ethnic insiders and perceived outsiders are likely to sharpen rather than transform into a global citizenship. Resource competition has made "nativeness" an important criterion of entitlement. Passports and migration laws have become the last bastion of a "hollowed-out sovereignty" of the nation state. Yet global epidemics, like COVID-19, which do not know borders or ethnicity, have also strengthened nation states, by repatriating citizens from around the world to come "home" where they would be cared for.

Patriotism manifests itself in the collective rituals that express pride in one's country. The singing of the national anthem or the display of the flag signals loyalty. Compared with Europe, Canada, or South Africa, the United States is widely considered a particularly patriotic nation, despite or because of the fact that the state is historically made up of immigrants from all parts of the world. Newcomers from different traditions are politically assimilated through unifying patriotic symbols.

In so far as patriotism engenders collective solidarity with fellow citizens and loyalty to the laws and democratic constitution, it is a positive and useful attitude. True patriotism fosters social responsibility and expects civic courage to defend the rights and freedoms that a democratic political culture bestows. As previously pointed out, the German philosopher Jürgen Habermas speaks of "constitutional patriotism," a pride in the rule of law, and constitutional guarantees, not ethnic affinity, as the emotional glue that should hold a multiethnic society together. Problems arise when one group of residents claim themselves to be the "true patriots" and aim at discriminating against immigrants and newcomers as untrustworthy "traitors" or "intruders." In Quebec the term "Pure Laine" has been used to distinguish those with exclusively French Canadian ancestry in contrast to the newcomers. Immigrants and newcomers are then relegated to the bottom of the "hierarchy of belonging."

In this situation patriotism becomes a double-edged sword that comprises both positive and dangerously negative attitudes. In the name of true patriotism intolerance toward dissent is frequently propagated, freedom of speech is restricted, and an arbitrary consensus is imposed. The very accusation of "unpatriotic behavior" intimidates teachers and students into self-censorship. They bow to conformity pressure that emanates from powerful media and authority prescriptions of what is legitimate and what is out of bounds and "politically incorrect." Nobody likes to be ostracized and marginalized as an outsider to the national consensus. In the United States, particularly after the national trauma of 9/11 and the ill-named Patriot Act, many members of certain religious and ethnic minorities suddenly found themselves labeled suspects, regardless of their individual loyalties. During the 1950s, Republican Senator Joseph McCarthy went on a similar collective crusade against alleged communist traitors in the ensuing Cold War.

To guard against such abuse of patriotism, teachers need not shy away from fostering national identity, let alone embrace Samuel Johnson's dictum that love of country is "the last refuge of a scoundrel." Teachers need to emphasize *critical patriotism.* This approach eschews the popular motto "my country, right or wrong!" Critical patriotism encourages pride in the "right," but engages equally forcefully with the "wrong." The very foundation of an open society is based on critical discourse in which nobody can claim a monopoly of truth and patriotism. Teachers therefore not only require knowledge in social studies or even tolerance toward unpopular opinions, but an attitude that nurtures autonomy and questioning of conventional wisdom among their subjects. As Henry Giroux (1983) has persuasively argued: "The real crisis in schools and youth culture may not be about censorship, freedom of speech, or other alleged evils of political correctness, but whether students are learning how to think critically, engage larger social issues, take risks, and develop a sense of social responsibility and civic courage" (p. 181).

Cosmopolitanism refers to a mindset curious about the world everywhere, an orientation of openness and broad-mindedness that transcends the narrow confines of one's own group, be it locality, religion, ethnicity, or nationality. Cosmopolitans perceive of themselves as citizens of the world. Martha Nussbaum (2019) defines their primary allegiance "to the community of human beings in the entire world" rather than their own national citizens. Cosmopolitans are ready to immerse themselves in other cultures, engage with difference, and acquire diverse "cultural capital." Nussbaum contrasts cosmopolitan universalism and internationalism with parochial ethnocentrism and inward-looking patriotism. She extends "an invitation to be an exile from the comfort of patriotism and its easy sentiments." In opposition to Richard Rorty's (1998) emphasis on shared American traditions, these cosmopolitans do not "rejoice in our American identity," but celebrate a "politics of difference" or pluralism, very much as Canada defines itself.

Advocates of cosmopolitanism rightly inveigh against an educational system that at best leaves students indifferent toward others beyond national borders and at worst ignorant about the outside world. A majority of adult Americans do not own a passport, which could be interpreted as their having little desire to explore other countries. However, cosmopolitanism need not be opposed to a critical patriotism. Pride in one's own heritage can be reconciled with appreciating other traditions. A reflective national or ethnic identity does not preclude a cosmopolitan outlook, and may even be a prerequisite for a broader perspective. Politically, the slogan "think globally, act locally" best expresses a useful strategic synthesis. The case for cosmopolitanism can be argued on moral as well as on pragmatic utilitarian grounds in an intertwined world. In the Kantian tradition cosmopolitans universalize moral obligations and advocate international solidarity. In Nussbaum's (2019) words: "If we really believe that all human beings are created equal and endowed with certain inalienable rights, we are morally required to think about what that conception requires us to do with and for the rest of the world" (p. 47). The treatment of noncitizens as neighbors puts this imperative to the test.

Cosmopolitanism in practice, as opposed to this noble, idealistic theory, however, faces two major obstacles: (1) Despite economic globalization, the world is still organized into nation-states. As has been elaborated previously, none of the 200 sovereign states has open borders that would allow people from everywhere to live anywhere without passports and permissions. The rich societies refuse to share their wealth with their poorer neighbors or even with their "fellow" poor nationals out of sheer greed. Our entire institutions militate against international solidarity and shape mindsets that are focused on the national good, the locality, ethnicity, or family. (2) If sociobiologists are correct, this selfishness of our species rests on evolutionary conditioning. According to this controversial view, people always prefer kin over nonkin, because such nepotism provided an evolutionary advantage in the competition for scarce resources. Survival depended on looking after your own first. Sociobiologists, like Pierre van den Berghe (1981), posit that ethnocentrism is universal, while racism is not. Van den Berghe (personnal communication, January 15, 2013) clarifies that xenophobia is not a necessary concomitant to ethnocentrism, but much stronger, with the additional element of competition. However, "the biological predisposition is to favor kin over non-kin, not to hate non-kin. Barring adverse experiences, cautious indifference and curiosity are more the norm toward strangers than hatred or fear, leaving open the possibility of a mutually profitable relationship of reciprocity." If this view is correct, then local–immigrant relations can also be improved by mutually beneficial reciprocity, according to van den Berghe. (ibid)

It is doubtful, however, whether nationalist and ethnocentrist attitudes serve the same useful purposes in an integrated world, where events in the remotest parts affect the rest of the globe. When the tropical rain forests are denuded, the climate everywhere changes. New diseases, like SARS or COVID-19, rapidly spread. Pollution of the air, terrorism, or migration because of poverty and civil wars do not stop at artificial borders. Isolationism is an option no longer.

This interconnectedness of the modern world requires international cooperation and global planning. People with a cosmopolitan mindset are better equipped for these complex tasks than parochial persons, who are comfortable only in their own culture and are oblivious of other people's ways of being. We are all inexorably entangled with the rest of the world. Based on sheer self-interest, it behooves us all to master the cosmopolitan cultural and political competencies to deal with this role with moral responsibility and strategic savvy.

How does one infuse minds socialized in narrow communalism, parochialism, or sectarianism with a necessary cosmopolitan outlook? An effective approach is critical introspection about tradition in each in-group. Once problematic aspects of celebrated traditions are questioned, students are no longer captives of their socialization. The transformation into autonomous, reasoning citizens is set in motion.

In the African tradition, the questioning could start with *ukuthwala,* the rural practice of abducting young women. Originally, it aimed at inducing the two families to negotiate the terms of a consensual marriage, but has deteriorated into powerful older men raping the abducted females and thereby branding them as property. The whole patriarchal tradition of gender inequality could find resonance among a susceptible African learner's audience, and applies to all other groups as well. It should include the still prevalent North and East African tradition of clitorectomy, fortunately not practiced in South Africa, as well as the circumcision of young men in initiation camps. Are there alternatives, in the case of the latter, where death from infection and injuries would be minimized? In the Indian tradition, the Hindu caste system could be the ideal subject for scrutiny. Although the caste order has been abandoned by the indentured laborers imported into Natal by the British colonial authorities, the 140 million Dalit outcasts still suffer from a customary tradition despite being outlawed in India. Other topics for critical analysis of tradition could focus on attitudes to gender, the merits and disadvantages of nonconsensual arranged marriages, the dowry system, and the role of family honor when endogamy is violated.

South Africa provides a case study of whether and when political struggles become ethnicized, or vice versa, when various cultural traditions become racialized and mobilized for political ends. At the same time, the tenacity of racial ideologies is tested when racism becomes dysfunctional in an interdependent economy. The legal deracialization in the face of increasing costs (sanctions, industrial action, illegitimacy) suggests a surprising rational choice in favor of a redefinition of a former racial identity. Ethnic identity was not abandoned, but pragmatically readjusted to fit changing circumstances. In its self-perception, the National Party (NP) negotiated itself *into* power, not *out* of power. Both sides claimed victory in the negotiations: the ANC for having achieved power through the ballot box; the NP for having locked the ANC into a Western liberal democracy and secured the survival of the capitalist order.

Political literacy could culminate in the question: What was liberation supposed to mean beyond equal rights? The ANC has not solved the tension between altering the economic structure radically or merely populating a colonial economy with those previously excluded. Built on comparatively cheap labor and the migratory labor system, the colonial economy has endured, regardless of who sits in corporate boardrooms. What has changed is that the unrest and gross inequality flowing from this condition is policed by a new regime—an ingenious "solution" for the old illegitimate ruling class. However, given the constraints of a global economic order and South Africa's dependency on this system, was there any realistic alternative? When students grasp these intricate connections between the local and the global, they have achieved a truly cosmopolitan consciousness.

What you have read in this chapter comprises the underlying assumptions and goals of my teaching and writings in different settings. I consider these assertions in the field of ethnic studies and political sociology to be valid universally, but their form of conveyance depends on the circumstances and audience.

I consider the ultimate result of political literacy to be open-mindedness, which should be appreciated in all democracies. Its opposite, dogmatism and fanaticism, belongs to authoritarian and totalitarian societies. With an open-minded outlook, active participation in the democratic polity is encouraged and moral responsibility initiated. We need the Friday Movement for policy changes on climate change and many other global concerns. This represents cosmopolitanism in action.

Conclusion

Lessons Learned From Five Different Countries for Teaching Political Literacy

To summarize and synthesize my life story in five different countries, I must necessarily simplify. Here I can only sketch some turning points and lessons to be drawn.

With my ancestors emigrating as indentured laborers to Natal, my South African–born parents shielded us as children from apartheid humiliations. I was culturally socialized with a strong Indian identity but avoided the trap of "tribalism" or racial distrust. Several studies in the American context (Huguley et al., 2019; Wang et al., 2020) highlight greater self-esteem, higher academic outcomes, and better mental health of minorities through ethnic socialization. The Indian community had little choice but to be self-reliant. Upward social mobility through higher education has since morphed almost into a family obligation in many Indian homes.

In my case, a parent-encouraged 2-year study experience in the United States, with the help of a scholarship from the Institute of International Education, resulted in a master's degree (1965). My first U.S. sojourn exposed me to the civil rights movement. With an enhanced political consciousness, I then faced a second border crossing upon returning to South Africa. Being in a secret illegal relationship with a visiting German academic, who was to become my fiancé, made us vulnerable to arrest under the Immorality Act. The writing was on the wall when university authorities were pressured by "forces beyond their control" for "non-academic reasons" to terminate my contract as a lecturer. It was clearly time to leave when Heribert received a letter that his visa would not be renewed and he should leave the country. After living in Germany for the better part of a year, we moved a second time in 1968 to English-speaking Canada to realize my dream of obtaining a PhD. Heribert, respecting how much this meant to me, gave up his job offer at the Frankfurt Institute. Before finally settling down as bourgeois academics with children, a house, and mortgage in comfortable Vancouver, we took the opportunity to spend 2 years in the Middle East (Cairo, 1972–1974) at the American University (AUC) and travelled widely in Israel, Lebanon, Syria, and Jordan. In between was a semester of teaching in Salisbury/Harare (1973), then called the University of Rhodesia, arranged by the liberal sociologist Marshall Murphry.

During the slow demise of apartheid we were again admitted as couple to South Africa. We institutionalized annual visits for research as well as family reasons. Our two daughters had married South African husbands from the Jewish community there. My mother, aged 105, still lives in Durban. On the way, we always spent several weeks in Berlin and Frankfurt with the German side of the family and old friends. This had been a pattern throughout our lives when the children were younger, so that they could have authentic experiences of the different components of their widespread family.

Selecting the most important lessons learned from living in all these areas may be useful for educators interested in applied political literacy. In summary, I identify the major problems or features of these settings as follows: colonialism in Southern Africa; melting pot ideology in the United States; migrancy and memory in Germany; multiculturalism, Quebec secessionism, and First Nations in Canada; and sectarianism in the Middle East.

SOUTH AFRICA

South Africa's overall problem is decolonization in a multiethnic divided society, still burdened by the legacy of apartheid. That means coming to terms with a complex history and making sense of its various components. History cannot be unscrambled.

Many analysts expected a race war during the 1980s. It was averted by a cooperating leadership on both sides. Mandela's gestures of reconciliation together with the hope of a better future in a nonracial democracy soothed the anger of Blacks during many breakdowns in negotiations. The White side under F.W. de Klerk calculated rationally that the costs of ongoing suppression were not sustainable in the long run. The National Party ceded political power, provided Whites retained and shared economic power. A neo-liberal constitution sealed this compromise.

However, the new ruling elite under Mandela's successors engaged in maladministration, corruption, and self-enrichment to such an extent that the previous inequality deepened. Reracialization is now growing together with emigration of White and Indian professionals.

Lesson: Peaceful transformation from a racialized society to a non-racial democracy is possible. It requires placing the national good ahead of party interest and selfish concerns by a rational leadership.

Reflecting on the labels used to construct and segregate culturally different as well as phenotypically similar population groups reveals the complex decolonization effort. I use racial and ethnic labels critically, not to reproduce the apartheid classifications. The problematic descriptions are part of the history and are now also officially used for measuring the success of affirmative action policies.

Informally, many people still identify with the imposed labels. *Blacks*, formerly labelled Bantu, are the African inhabitants. This 80% majority considers itself indigenous. However, that distinction is also claimed by the few surviving San (hunters and gatherers, "Bushmen") and Khoisan (herders). Out of this mixture, plus imported slaves and European settlers, evolved *Coloreds*, people of mixed origin (9%). The overwhelming majority of Coloreds are culturally very similar to White Afrikaners, being Calvinists in religion and Afrikaans in language. *Indians* or *Asians* (3%) and *Whites* (8%) form the rest of what are now referred to as "minorities." The derogatory label *Non-White* was rejected by Biko's Black Consciousness movement and replaced with "Black" for all three discriminated groups: Blacks, Coloreds, and Indians. It was difficult to unify all three groups under this category, because they were differentially oppressed.

In accordance with the ANC Freedom Charter of 1958, everyone who lives in the country legally and identifies with it as a homeland, is politically an African, regardless of culture and race. The underlying issue is no longer skin color, but entitlement and economic claims based on group classification and past disadvantage. The new hierarchy of advantage is Black, Colored, Indian, and White. In this regard, Colored and Indians often say that they were not White enough before and now they are not Black enough.

THE UNITED STATES

The United States legally achieved self-determination and independence from England after a war, and also abolished slavery. In my experience, the problem is the vast discrepancy between legal equality and a contrary reality. The United States defined itself as a "melting pot."

Lesson: Instead of "melting," the country has not overcome its ingrained racism, despite a sizeable Black bourgeoisie and a first Black president. Nowadays a predominant nation of immigrants paradoxically fights a war against new immigrants having the "wrong" origin or religion.

I would identify three major differences between the racial strife in the United States and South Africa. Unlike the struggle that a *minority* of African Americans fought during a similar period over civil rights, in South Africa a *majority* of the population was racialized. Whereas the U.S. national government intervened on the side of African Americans, the South African regime legislated ever harsher racial discrimination. In the United States, legal equality for the minority did not threaten the national order. In South Africa enfranchisement of the majority meant regime change. From this perspective, the U.S. civil rights conflict was easier to solve, while in South Africa the shift of political power, and potentially economic wealth posed greater obstacles. In addition, cultural differences, such as language and religion, in the United States were minimal and the African American middle class at least had already melted into mainstream ways of life and consumption habits.

GERMANY

The history of no other European society was marred by such infamy as Nazi Germany. The annihilation of some 6 million Jews throughout occupied Europe as well as the murder of political dissidents, disabled people, homosexuals, Roma/Sinti, and Russian prisoners of war, was unique. Yet the country with the most horrid past has also dealt with it in a remarkable way, as pointed out earlier.

Lesson: Fully acknowledging collective crimes in all spheres of life, making it the center of a new political culture, assuming responsibility and paying restitution for the sins of forebears, is widely admired. Above all, reeducating following generations about the past reveals considerable impact. With laws criminalizing anti-constitutional activity and political leadership across the political spectrum establishing a consensus, the country is now less prone to the reemergence of fascism, despite the rise of neo-Nazi fringe groups. The new right faces a strong barrier of resistance, particularly among the younger generation. Their cosmopolitan consciousness, however, has only partially affected national attitudes toward the "new Jews": the refugees and economic migrants from the global South. Practicing an open border policy for a short while in 2015 has cost the government dearly in losing a sizeable conservative voting block.

In a divided Germany during the Cold War, about 2.5 million mostly skilled workers had moved from East to West Germany before 1961, when the East German government sealed the open border with establishing the Berlin Wall and extending the Iron Curtain through the country. A shortage of labor necessitated waves of foreign economic migrants, referred to as "guest workers," for rebuilding West Germany. The guests adapted to the host country and stayed. Initially restricted to individual workers, family reunification followed. First- and second-generation economic migrants gradually lost their cultural background and assimilated. Yet they were still stigmatized as having a "migration background." In contrast to the first wave of Southern Europeans, integration of Turks into the mainstream was hampered by their recruitment in rural Turkey and a different religion. Moreover, until recently, Germany stuck to the myth of return by the "guests."

The heated German discourse, similar to the United Kingdom and Eastern Europe, centers upon two contrasting views of identity. The traditional vision sees collective identity as necessary for national cohesion. It is anchored in nostalgia for a romanticized past of order and trust derived from ethnic homogeneity and unifying values. I hold an opposing vision of identity as something private, individual, and self-chosen, without denying the invasive role of the way others see us. According to the late sociologist Ulrich Beck, there are 80 million ways to be German. For him, like Jürgen Habermas, heritage identity (Herkunftsidentitaet), pride in the homeland (Heimat), and belonging to a cherished place and culture, can be combined with "transnational identity." This means a cosmopolitan commitment to be "your brother's keeper" rather than caring only for the national kin. I believe that the nepotism of kin preference actually disadvantages and holds nations back in a postnational world. In an interconnected global marketplace, welcoming newcomers, risk-takers, and innovators does not amount to "giving your nation away." If we look at successful immigration societies like the United States and Canada, they profit enormously from the ongoing intake of foreigners.

CANADA

In contrast to the melting pot ideology of the United States, Canada defines itself as multicultural. The difference is often exaggerated, and several commentators deny it altogether. Two respected Canadian sociologists, Jeffrey Reitz and Raymond Breton (1994) have, in fact, titled their book *The Illusion of Difference: Realities of Ethnicity in Canada and the United States*. The American historian George M. Fredrickson (1999) concludes: "Despite the myths that Canada is a 'mosaic' and the United States a 'melting pot,' racial prejudice and xenophobia exist to about the same extent in both countries" (p. 32). This may be argued.

Lesson: While there exists resentment toward newcomers in some conservative circles, the fundamental Canadian problem remains the potential secessionism of several subnations.

A fundamentally different political order in Canada contrasts sharply with the U.S. system of governance. Several differences stand out: Firstly, Canada admits twice as many immigrants annually per capita (0.9%) than the United States. Secondly, Canadians are represented by several political parties in parliament. The Westminster electoral system of first-past-the-post compels all parties to move to the center to court the immigrant vote, broaden their appeal, and avoid the polarization of two parties as in the presidential system of the United States. Thirdly, Canada is much more of a welfare state in the North European sense. Everybody has access to identical medical services, even if they are unable to pay. Fourthly, multiculturalism exists alongside multilingualism with two official languages. Also, people speak in their nonofficial mother tongues in public without being frowned upon. Fifthly, strong federalism is guaranteed by the existence of Quebec, which would otherwise secede. "Reasonable accommodation" of cultural/ethnic conflicts is proclaimed as the method of consensus aspirations. Finally, about 600 First Nations make slow progress in land restitution, self-government, and setting their own priorities.

The threat of subnational conflict, particularly the existence of Quebec and the potential for secession, constitutes both the problem and the safeguard of compromise and ethnic diversity.

EGYPT AND THE MIDDLE EAST

Egypt is riven by historical tensions between a Sunni Muslim majority and 20% Christian Copts, as well as between Islamists (Muslim Brotherhood) and secularists. Religious differences overlay class divides, with the minority Copts be-ing on average wealthier and better educated than the impoverished Sunni major-ity. Similar sectarian issues split Israel internally and externally between Jews and Palestinians in the West Bank and Gaza. Twenty percent of the Arabs in Israel live as second-class citizens in an official Jewish state. In Lebanon, Christians, Sunnis, and Shiite Muslims (Hezbollah) erupt in repeated civil wars. Although officially in a power-sharing government, the factions resemble feudal warlords in an uneasy truce more than a stable democracy. In Syria, a Shiite minority of 20% Alawites brutally dominates a Sunni majority. After the overthrow of Saddam Hussein, a Sunni president in Iraq, the Shiite majority took power with American support. All these domestic problems are overshadowed by the two regional superpowers: feudal Saudi Arabia manipulating the Sunni factions, and clerical Iran supporting Shiite factions with arms. In addition the United States and Russia defend their proxies in the region.

Lesson: Sectarian conflicts are generally nonnegotiable because religious dog-ma represents an absolute which is not bargainable.

On various visits to Israel, when I worked on our coauthored book *Seeking Mandela: Peacemaking Between Israelis and Palestinians* (Adam & Moodley, 2005), the nonnegotiable nature of religiously entrenched positions was reinforced. This struck me when standing before the Wailing Wall in Jerusalem. Wise men on both sides confirmed it. I felt despondent. When visiting India, I remember a similar sentiment when Hindus in Ayodhya insisted that a mosque must be torn down be-cause once there was a Hindu temple on the same sacred spot. When two gods are born in the same place, you cannot share it. Why can Jerusalem with the Al Aqsa mosque and the Wailing Wall just 100 meters below not become an international holy city, shared by all religions? All religious dogmatists claim a monopoly of truth. Philosopher Karl Popper in his 1945 book *The Open Society and Its Enemies* asserts that in his liberal utopia nobody owns a monopoly of truth. I am much more comfortable with Popper's view that history is an ongoing argument. I aban-doned interest in the Middle East because sectarian conflicts are truly intractable.

CONCLUDING INSIGHTS

Looking at the multifaceted nature of ethnic divides in general have provided me with several sobering insights.

During 3 months in early 1994, when South Africans were celebrating the release of Mandela, about 800,000 people were massacred in Rwanda at a rate that surpassed the industrialized death camps of the Nazis, despite mostly low-tech killing by machete. As Gourevitch (1998) has described it, they had been "neigh-bors, schoolmates, colleagues, sometimes friends, even in-laws" (p. 180). The ma-jority Hutu population and the minority Tutsis spoke the same language, belonged to the same (mostly Roman Catholic) religion, and lived side by side. From this I learned that social integration, interethnic mixing, and even successful assimilation of minorities into majority cultures do not guarantee intergroup harmony.

Another example demonstrates this. Before the rise of the Nazis, secularized German Jews were fully integrated into German society, indistinguishable in lifestyles, outlook, attitudes, citizenship, and appearance from other Germans. Yet, like Tutsis in Rwanda, they were singled out by a nationalistic majority for genocide on the basis of an assumed different ancestry and an imagined global conspiracy.

Psychoanalysts argue that the repressed unconscious can be projected outward (R. Koenigsberg, 1977). Fantasy and daydreams have been transferred into reality. Despite Jews constituting less than 0.5% of the total German population, the Hitler propaganda of a virus contaminating the corporate body of a healthy *volk* had persuaded 37% in the last free election in 1933. The German and Rwandan examples of genocide and mass violence were not unique exceptions. They have been repeated on different scales and with varied rationalizations in many parts of the world and can be triggered in the future. Even a peace optimist like Martin Luther King once wrote in reflections on prominent Nazi victim Reinhold Niebuhr: "Instead of assured progress in wisdom and decency, man faces the ever present possibility of a swift relapse not merely to animalism, but into such calculated cruelty as no other animal can practice."

When a minority has been set up for unequal treatment, it has little to do with its own behavior. It is often targeted, regardless of its desires to assimilate or separate. We need to look at the collective predisposition of the dominant group to understand, why one segment can be easily mobilized to turn against another segment of the population. Above all, the actions of political elites and opinion leaders are crucial in inciting aggressive behavior. What needs to be remembered is that they are working with social forces present within the society, and not creating a genocidal situation out of a vacuum.

Ethnic antagonism is also not caused by high numbers of perceived strangers. All too easily an economistic reductionism lists heightened competition or conflicting material interests as the real causes of ethnic strife. While discrimination obviously benefits some and shortchanges others, it would be misleading to reduce ethnic antagonism to material privileging alone. For example, former East Germany experienced many more incidents of violent xenophobia despite a relatively small number of resident foreigners (100,000) compared with West Germany with a 45 times greater population of foreigners (4.5 million) competing for scarce jobs. As a Polish saying goes, there can be virulent anti-Semitism without any Jews left in a country.

Historically oppressed groups do not necessarily eschew the same behavior once they have gained power themselves. Historical victimhood does not immunize against repeating similar abuses of others. Large sections of the new South African political elite misappropriated for self-enrichment public funds that could have benefitted the poor.

This rather pessimistic outlook, based on solid historical evidence, can serve as a useful "reality principle." However, it should not deter politically conscious educators from exploring alternatives. If the psychological roots of the appeal of ethnonational identity are recognized, then other attractive identities can also be imagined. Multiple identities are becoming more important in all parts of the world. My autobiography exudes hope and shows how obstacles are overcome. The power of new ideas and human agency remain at least as strong as economic interests. What Max Weber called "ideal interests" knows no borders.

Afterword

Writing a memoir helps put a life in perspective. It creates space for reflecting on one's aspirations, trajectories, disappointments, and achievements. For educators, it can also make explicit what might have been unexamined philosophies of teaching and research. And for readers, a memoir can provide, if not a roadmap for their own lives, at least a catalyst for thinking about what they believe and how they've tried to put their beliefs into practice. In this memoir, universally renowned scholar of sociology and education Kogila Moodley has invited readers into her life, in the process giving us a more complete picture of her much admired work in diversity and global civic education and a nuanced understanding of pre- and post-apartheid South Africa.

The granddaughter of Indian indentured laborers brought to Natal, South Africa in the 1860s, Kogila Moodley grew up in Durban and came of age in the 1950s and 1960s just as a serious pushback to apartheid was starting. She describes her family as members of "a middle group," that is, neither the most privileged White "settlers," nor indigenous Blacks, the most oppressed group in a highly hierarchical and racist society. While living with some of the trappings and aspirations of middle-class life, she and her family members nevertheless experienced displacement, inferior schooling, and other indignities associated with the oppressive conditions of apartheid. Besides the race-based laws governing education, housing, work, and other aspects of life, less flagrant but no less repressive traditions and rules made existence arduous for most. For example, when she and the love of her life, Heribert, a German scholar visiting South Africa, began courting in the late 1960s, they could never be alone in a car or apartment for fear of being arrested under the odious Immorality Act. Moodley would go on to a distinguished academic career, albeit primarily outside of South Africa. In her story, one can see the effects of the repulsive laws and traditions in a society where nearly everyone suffered some level of profound psychic, emotional, and physical damage, although, of course, to differing degrees. The memoir chronicles Moodley's remarkable journey from a socially sanctioned pecking order in housing, education, and life in general, to her future as an internationally respected academic. Following her through education and travels in South Africa, Germany, the United States, the Middle East, Canada, and across the world, we learn not only about the woman, but also about the fascinating context in which she has lived.

There is much to be learned from this insightful memoir. I limit my comments to those that are especially relevant for educators, who I assume will be the majority of readers—although I certainly hope that it will reach a far wider readership who can also learn from Moodley's numerous insights on culture, race, colonialism, and history. The book underscores that no nation has a monopoly on injustice, although some including South Africa certainly have been more cruel and unjust than others. But it is not alone. Reading the author's reflections on the indignities of life for the most subjugated members of her society, I couldn't help but compare these examples to the repression of different segments of the U.S. population, from conquered indigenous people to enslaved Africans to colonized Mexicans, Puerto Ricans, and Filipinos. Though different in scope and degree, the similarities with U.S. slavery, *de jure* and *de facto* segregation, and the repellant Jim Crow era laws are particularly revealing: The enforced servitude, the use of passbooks, even after slavery was abolished (see, for example, Madigan, 2013, on the aftermath of the 1921 Tulsa riots), the assignment of toilets and other amenities according to race, the enforcement of "sundown towns" as comprehensively documented by James Loewen (Loewen, 2018), and the more recent mass incarceration of Blacks, or what Michelle Alexander has called "the new Jim Crow" (Alexander, 2010). Even *Applesamy and Naidoo,* a South African radio program that Moodley describes as the "trivial chatter of two Indian men," is reminiscent of *Amos 'n' Andy,* the supposedly good-natured yet fundamentally racist U.S. radio, and later, television program of roughly the same era.

For educators, Moodley's pungent commentaries on elementary and secondary schools and universities based on group membership—where people are still classified as White, Indian, Colored, or Black—are particularly jarring. But scratching just below the surface of our own history, the similarities are evident: the author describes how South African students were subjected to "sanitized knowledge which had little to do with our everyday worlds," a description that could equally describe the education of marginalized populations in U.S. schools. This memoir also makes clear that the field of diversity writ large, which includes multicultural education, is a worldwide phenomenon, not simply limited to the United States. In fact, it has found a home in many other societies as well, albeit mostly in Western democracies. For those who inspired her own education and life, Moodley acknowledges Mahatma Gandhi, whose transformation as an international leader in passive resistance began while he lived in South Africa, and Nelson Mandela, a native son, both of whom deeply influenced her ideas and career. At the same time, she chronicles some of her many international colleagues in education, sociology, and anthropology, including her long-standing friendship and academic relationship with James Banks, the dean of the multicultural education movement whose interest in civic global education mirrors her own.

As a former professor of multicultural teacher education, I found Moodley's descriptions of pedagogy in the courses she taught on race, ethnicity, and culture particularly compelling. Although I've certainly had a fulfilled life as a researcher, it was my work as a teacher and mentor that were most gratifying. Her depictions of interactions with her students remind me why I loved teaching preservice and practicing teachers about these same topics. Moreover, her sage comments about the various traps associated with the teaching and research on diversity are worthwhile for all educators to heed. While deeply appreciating the benefits of cultural affirmation, for example, she also understands the pitfalls of an uncritical stance toward culture. She writes, for example, that "the chauvinistic glorification of culture can become a straitjacket of conformity pressure that stifles individual imagination."

Although not specifically related to education, Chapter 7, where Moodley recounts her relationship with Heribert, her husband of several decades, is especially sweet. A courtship in South Africa was not easy, and her statement, "Needless to say, the relationship was growing under the most trying of circumstances," is one of the great understatements in the book. But there is humor here as well: She writes, "Even walking down the street together elicited looks by both Blacks and Whites, which made us feel as if we were walking in our underwear." Her commentary on this relationship explores how two people of vastly different backgrounds and histories can fall deeply in love and share a life despite those differences. She reminds us that focusing on differences alone can sometimes hide the many similarities that people also share. Besides the most important aspect of her relationship with Heribert—that is, raising their children—the author also highlights the many interests that have bound them together over the years: a love of culture, a curiosity about the world, and an open mind.

Near the beginning of the book, Moodley shares her hope that in writing her memoir she hopes to promote a more global political literacy through storytelling. And indeed, stories are ever-present in the book, from childhood memories of generosity and love in her large extended family to depictions of South Africa that go beyond the sociopolitically unjust conditions in which the majority were forced to live, to encompassing global stories of a fascinating mix of people, customs, and societies. Moodley begins her memoir by making it clear that she is more comfortable with the genre of academic writing that has been her *forté* for many years rather than with memoir, a new genre for her. Yet, her many stories of quotidian family life, her fond recollections of childhood and young adulthood despite the humiliations of apartheid, the touching description of falling in love with Heribert and their subsequent life together, her evocative descriptions of life in Frankfurt, Cairo, and Vancouver, among other places: all these make it obvious that she has managed to conquer this new genre as well.

The book builds up to the final chapters in which Moodley explores what she means by global political literacy and its hopes for a more just education and, by implication, a more humane society. Given the first nine chapters of the book, readers may find the abrupt change in tone in the final two chapters, particularly in Chapter 11, unsettling. But this is the chapter where Moodley puts on her academic hat, the one with which she's most at home, and where she uses her professional voice to share some of the many lessons she has learned in the places where she has lived in the hope that readers, no matter how different their own experiences may be, can learn. She extols the virtues of what she calls political literacy which, as she writes, "to some extent immunizes against racist temptations." All readers can learn from her thoughts on critical introspection, cosmopolitanism, civic education, and the need for open-mindedness, all of which would help promote a more just education regardless of the society in which one lives.

Chapter 11 will be of special interest to educators who work in diverse settings and who are eager to help their students of whatever age or education level become politically literate. The chapter, aptly titled "Political Literacy as Strategy to Combat Bigotry," includes her reflections on citizenship and what it means beyond the borders of South Africa or of any particular nation. A celebration of her life, this memoir is also an acknowledgement that, as is true for all of us, Kogila Moodley did not get here on her own but only with the love and generosity of her family and the careful guidance of mentors, colleagues, and friends. Throughout the previous chapters, Moodley has proven her humanity, but it is in this chapter that her wisdom shines through. It is here where the lessons she has learned, although in different places around the world, become universal for all educators regardless of where or whom they teach. Eminently readable and engaging, this memoir is at once poetic, wise, and erudite.

Sonia Nieto
Professor Emerita, Language, Literacy, and Culture
College of Education
University of Massachusetts, Amherst

REFERENCES

Alexander, M. (2010). *The new Jim Crow: Mass incarceration in the age of colorblindness.* The New Press.

Loewen, J. W. (2018). *Sundown towns: A hidden dimension of American racism.* The New Press.

Madigan, T. (2013). *The burning: Massacre, destruction, and the race riot of 1921.* Thomas Dunne Books.

References

Adam, H. (1971). *Modernizing racial domination.* California University Press.

Adam, H., & Giliomee, H. (1979). *Ethnic power mobilized: Can South Africa change?* Yale University Press

Adam, H., & Moodley, K. (1986). *South Africa without apartheid: Dismantling racial domination.* University of California Press.

Adam, H., & Moodley, K. (2005). *Seeking Mandela: Peacemaking between Israelis and Palestinians.* Temple University Press.

Adam, H., & Moodley, K. (2015). *Imagined liberation: Xenophobia, citizenship, and identity in South Africa, Germany, and Canada.* Temple University Press.

Adam, H., Slabbert, V. Z., & Moodley, K. (1997). *Comrades in business: Post-liberation politics in South Africa.* Tafelberg.

Adorno, T.W., Frenkel-Brunswik, E., Levinson, D. J., & Sanford, R. N. (1950) *The authoritarian personality.* Harpers.

Ancer, J. (2019). *Betrayal: The secret lives of apartheid spies.* Tafelberg.

Banks, J. A. (1997). *Educating citizens in a multicultural society.* Teachers College Press.

Coll, C. G., Lamberty, G., Jenkins, R., McAdoo, H. P., Crnic, K., Wasik, B. H., & Garcia, H. V. (1996). An integrative model for the study of developmental competencies in minority children. *Child Development, 67*(5), 1891–1914. http://dx.doi.org/10.2307/1131600

Cooke, R. (2015, October 11). Nawal El Saadawi: 'Do you feel you are liberated? I feel I am not.' the guardian.com/books/2015/oct/11/nawal-el-saadawi-interview-do-feel-you-are-liberated-not.

Crick, B. R. (2000). *Essays on citizenship.* Continuum.

Dlamini, J. (2009). *Native nostalgia.* Jacana Media.

Douglas, A. (2012). Educating for real and hoped for political worlds: Ways forward in developing political literacy. https://citeseerx.ist.psu.edu/viewdoc/download?doi=10.1.1.461.8017&rep=rep1&type=pdf

Dweck, C. S. (2016). *Mindset: The new psychology of success.* Random House.

Esterhuyse, W. (2012). *Endgame: Secret talks and the end of apartheid.* Tafelberg.

Fredrickson, G. M. (1999). Models of American ethnic relations: A historical perspective. In D. A. Prentice & D. T. Miller (Eds.), *Cultural divides: Understanding and overcoming group conflict* (pp. 23–34). Russell Sage Foundation.

Gandhi, M. K. (1927) *An autobiography. The story of my experiments with truth.* Navajivan Trust.

Gandhi, M. K. (1999). Speech to Gandhi Seva Sangh, Hubli, April 17, 1937. In *The collected works of Mahatma Gandhi*. Publications Division Government of India. https://www.gandhiashramsevagram.org/gandhi-literature/collected-works-of-mahatma-gandhi-volume-1-to-98.php

Giroux, H. A. (1983). *Theory and resistance in education: Towards a pedagogy for the opposition*. Bergin & Garvey.

Gourevitch, P. (1998). *We wish to inform you that tomorrow we will be killed with our families: Stories from Rwanda*. Farrar, Straus and Giroux.

Guha, R. (2013). *Gandhi before India*. Random House.

Habermas, J. (1998). *The inclusion of the other: Studies in political theory* (C. Cronin & P. De Greiff, Eds.). MIT Press.

Hall, M. (2013, December 12). Mandela saw education as a powerful weapon for freedom. *Times Higher Education*.

Hansard. (1959). 20,17 June 1959, cols 8318-8320, Government of South Africa.

Hardiman, D. (2004). *Gandhi in his time and ours: The global legacy of his ideas*. University of Natal Press.

Hiralal, K. (2010, August 15). Plucky sisters who dared to fight. *Sunday Tribune* (South Africa), 4. https://www.pressreader.com/south-africa/sunday-tribune-south-africa/20100815/282969626368036

Hjerm, M. (2001). Education, xenophobia and nationalism: A comparative analysis. *Journal of Ethnic and Migration Studies, 27*(1), 37–60.

hooks, b. (1996a) *Killing rage, ending racism*. Penguin.

hooks, b.(1996b) *Bone black: Memories of girlhood*. Holt.

Huguley, J. P., Wang, M., Vasquez, A. C., & Guo, J. (2019). Parental ethnic-racial socialization practices and the construction of children of color's ethnic-racial identity: A research synthesis and meta-analysis. *Psychological Bulletin, 145*(5), 437–458. https://doi.org/10.1037/bul0000187

King, M. L. (1994). The theology of Reinhold Niebuhr. In C. Carson, R. Luker, P. A. Russell, & P. Holloran (Eds.), *The papers of Martin Luther King, Jr. Volume II: Rediscovering Precious Values, July 1951–November 1955*. University of California Press at Berkeley and Los Angeles. https://kinginstitute.stanford.edu/king-papers/documents/theology-reinhold-niebuhr

Koenigsberg, R. (1977) *The psychoanalysis of racism, revolution and nationalism*. Library of Social Science.

Maharaj, M., & Kathrada, A. (2006). *Mandela: The authorized portrait*. Andrews Mc Meel Publ.

Mamdani, M. (1996). *Citizen and subject: Contemporary Africa and the legacy of late colonialism*. Princeton University Press.

Mandela, N. (1964). Speech from the Dock, Rivonia Trial. sbs.com.au/news/transcript-nelson-mandela-speech-I-am-prepared-to-die

Mandela, N. (1994). *Long walk to freedom*. Little Brown.

Mandela, N. (2011) *Conversations with myself*. Canada: Anchor

Milner, H. (2002). *Civic literacy: How informed citizens make democracy work*. University Press of New England.

Moodley, K. (1995). *African minorities and language, island positions.* Goree Institute, Goree Island, Senegal.

Moodley, K. (1999). Anti-racist education through political literacy: The case of Canada. In S. May (Ed.), *Critical multiculturalism: Rethinking multicultural and antiracist education* (pp. 138–152). Falmer Press.

Moodley, K. (2000). African renaissance and language policies in comparative perspective. *Politikon, 27*(1), 103–115. https://doi.org/10.1080/02589340050004127

Moodley, K. (2001). Ethnic strife and democracy. In N. Dorsen & P. Gifford (Eds.), *Democracy and the rule of law* (pp. 113–126). CQ Press.

Moodley, K. (2011). Canada as a divided society or as a model for ethnic cohesion? In T. Hanf, (Ed.), *The political function of education in deeply divided countries.* Nomos.

Ndebele, N. S. (1991). *Rediscovery of the ordinary: Essays on South African literature and culture.* COSAW.

Ndebele, N. S. (2007). *Fine lines from the box: Further thoughts about our country.* Umuzi.

Nussbaum, M. C. (2019). *The cosmopolitan tradition.* Belknap Press.

Okada, J. (1978). *No-no boy.* University of Washington Press.

Popper, K. (1945). *The open society and its enemies.* Routledge.

Reitz, J. G., & Breton, R. (1994). *The illusion of difference: Realities of ethnicity in Canada and the United States.* C. D. Howe Institute.

Rorty, R. (1998). *Achieving our country: Leftist thought in twentieth-century America.* Harvard University Press.

Sauerbrey, A. (2017, August 23). How Germany deals with neo-Nazis. *The New York Times.* https://www.nytimes.com/2017/08/23/opinion/germany-neo-nazis-charlottesville.html

Sen, A. (2009). *The idea of justice.* Harvard University Press

Smith, A. D. (1986). *The ethnic origin of nations.* Wiley-Blackwell.

Soudien, C. (2015). Curriculum, knowledge, and the idea of South Africa. *International Journal of Development Education and Global Learning, 7*(2), 26–45. https://doi.org/10.18546/IJDEGL.07.2.04

Stengel, R. (2012). *Nelson Mandela: Portrait of an extraordinary man.* Virgin Books.

Turner, R. (1972) *The eye of the needle: Towards participatory democracy in South Africa.* Seagull.

Van den Berghe, P. (1967). *Race and racism: A comparative perspective.* John Wiley & Sons.

Van den Berghe, P. (1981). *The ethnic phenomenon.* Elsevier.

Waldron, J. (2019, September 12). Quibbling, wrangling. [Review of the book *Revolutionary constitutions: Charismatic leadership and the rule of law,* by Bruce Ackerman]. *London Review of Books, 41*(17). https://www.lrb.co.uk/the-paper/v41/n17/jeremy-waldron/quibbling-wrangling

Wang, M., Henry, D. A., Smith, L. V., Huguley, J. P., & Guo, J. (2020). Parental ethnic-racial socialization practices and children of color's psychosocial and behavioral adjustment: A systematic review and meta-analysis. *American Psychologist, 75*(1),1–22. http://dx.doi.org/10.1037/amp0000464

Weinstein, R. S. (2002). *Reaching higher. The power of expectations in schooling.* Harvard University Press.

Index

About the Author

Kogila Moodley is professor emerita of the University of British Columbia, Vancouver and the first holder of the David Lam Chair in Multicultural Education. She has served as president of the International Sociological Association's Research Committee on Ethnic, Minority and Race Relations (1998–2002), as well as on the board of the leading journal *Ethnic and Racial Studies*.

Her books include *Imagined Liberation: Xenophobia, Citizenship and Identity in South Africa, Germany and Canada* (with H. Adam, 2015); *Seeking Mandela: Peacemaking Between Israelis and Palestinians* (with H. Adam, 2005); *Comrades in Business: Post-Liberation Politics in South Africa* (with H. Adam and F. Van Zyl Slabbert, 1998); *The Opening of the Apartheid Mind: Options for the New South Africa* (with H. Adam, 1993); *Democratizing South Africa: Challenges for Canadian Policy* (with H. Adam, 1992); *Beyond Multicultural Education: International Perspectives* (ed.,1992); *South Africa Without Apartheid: Dismantling Racial Domination* (with H. Adam, 1986); and *Race Relations and Multicultural Education* (1992).